It's OK

I've got Everything under control.

–God

To one who has faith, no explanation is necessary.
To one without faith, no explanation is possible.

Thomas Aquinas

Have you ever felt as if everything is slipping out of control? A situation comes at you seemingly from nowhere and throws all the other plans you've made completely out the window. And how about all those day-to-day quandaries that drive you to your wit's end? Or a calendar so jam-packed with things to do and places to go that you feel like you haven't got a moment to call your own?

That's when you most need to hear the message in this book—*It's OK, I've got everything under control. –God.*

On each page, there's a time honored quotation followed by a reflection to inspire and encourage you. From cover to cover, you'll find suggestions to help you regain control where you can and surrender control where you must. Most importantly, these words will remind you where real control lies—with God, who loves you with an all-encompassing love.

Yes, it's OK to feel out of control once in a while—because God already has complete control, and that's the greatest feeling of all!

A Pause for Perspective

Our competence comes from God.
2 Corinthians 3:5 NIV

Exhausted, you plop into bed, determined to leave the worries of the day behind you. You fall into a deep sleep, and then all too soon the alarm goes off. You lie awake a few minutes, steeling yourself to face the problem again—only to have the solution pop right into your mind! How could you have missed it yesterday?

When we're focused exclusively on problems so big, so formidable, so outside what we thought we'd ever have to confront, answers rarely come right away. A difficult medical diagnosis terrifies us…and only after some time has passed do we recall that our best friend came through the same thing a few years back. She's the perfect person to confide in! A star-player son or daughter is crushed not to have made the varsity team…we're shocked, but then later remember that the community team is looking for a talented, energetic coach. We're worried sick about our finances…yet as soon as we stop stressing and sit down with our budget, we determine where we can spend less and save more.

Though you may not have control over every problem that enters your life, a step away…a good night's sleep…a quiet prayer for God's guidance helps you find the way out. Today, treat yourself to a pause for perspective. Let God lead you to the solution that's hiding in plain sight.

Equipped to Control

We know that all things work together for good to them that love God.

Romans 8:28

"For peace of mind," someone once quipped, "resign as manager of the universe." Yet when it seems as if the world is spinning out of control, we'd give anything for a little say-so over the running of the universe! The truth remains, though, that we don't wield power over global events—or even our own circumstances, the people around us, or even ourselves much of the time. We just don't have absolute ability to change everything we see that's wrong with the world. More to the point, we weren't given absolute ability.

What we have been given, however, is this—the ability to think, do, and learn from personal experience and the experience of others. Though we aren't able to govern the world (what a load of problems that would be!), we are wonderfully equipped to add kindness and goodness to our corner of it. Each of us can choose a positive attitude no matter what life sends our way…to treat others with compassion and understanding, no matter how hard it is at times…to change things for the better whenever possible…to make constructive, life-affirming choices for ourselves and those who depend on us.

As for controlling the world and everything in it, including badly-behaved people and the tricky events of our lives? Let's leave that to God, who actually does possess what it takes to do it. After all, He really is manager of the universe!

Getting a Move-On

Do what you can,
with what you have, where you are.
Theodore Roosevelt

Let's do something! Without taking action, we can't expect to make a difference in our lives or change the situations that drive us to distraction. Untreated illnesses, for example, only worsen with time. Neglected relationships simply grow cold and slip away with the passage of time. Denied or ignored problems rarely vanish, but most often increase in significance and intensity. Most of us have learned these truths the hard way—through personal experience. Do something!

Yet doing something doesn't mean we're doing the right thing. Often we don't know what to do, so we're at a standstill until we can figure out our best course of action. Sometimes taking effective steps is impossible because we lack ability, power, or authority to make things happen. But significant events are under our control, and we can act on them whenever we're ready:

- Identify the problem or circumstance as objectively as possible.
- Recognize our emotions, feelings, and attitudes, and take responsibility for them.
- Remain open to changing the way we look at things.
- Commit ourselves to doing the best we can with what we have, regardless of our resources.
- Take timely and well-considered action, firmly believing that God will give us the strength to see things through.

Our desire for an outcome guaranteed? Forget it, because results ultimately belong to God. But we can do something—the right thing—and then leave the rest in His action-packed hands. He will see it to the finish.

There's an Off Button

Anxiety weighs down the heart.
Proverbs 12:25 NIV

At his college's orientation session for parents, Caleb's mom listened as the speaker pointed out how the pervasiveness of texting has changed how parents keep in touch. Instead of a once-a-week phone call, many parents check in with their students once, if not several times, every day. As if to prove the speaker's point, Caleb's mom noticed that most of the parents around her had their eyes fixed on their phones!

At session's end, parents were to join their students at lunch. Automatically, Caleb's mom reached for her cell, and that's when she panicked—her device was missing! Vanished! How could she reach Caleb to remind him to meet her in the dining hall for lunch? "And that's when it hit me," she said later. "I felt like it was God's way of making me realize that I don't need constant contact anymore. He could find his way to the dining hall without my help!"

The incident reminds her that she needs to loosen control so Caleb can start taking control of his life. Yes, after a frantic search through her purse and coat pockets, she located her cell phone—and its Off button!

It's not only parents of adult children, but all of us find it hard to let go of people, places, and memories that are close to our hearts. Yet there comes a time for us to press the Off button, move ahead, and let God take control, confident that He will.

The Spiritual Side of Money

If money be not thy servant, it will be thy master.

Francis Bacon

What's the one thing guaranteed to bring on a severe case of heartburn? A red-hot chili pepper for sure, but more often, money. Or the lack of it, that is. When prices skyrocket, bills pile up, and a boost in income isn't even on your radar screen, it's a stomach-churning time.

You might imagine that money isn't a spiritual topic—that God doesn't care about money—but it is very much a spiritual topic, and He definitely cares. In the Bible, people borrowed, lent, spent, and saved money. While some hoarded it, others shared it. Some lived in luxury, others in poverty. Some controlled it, others let it control them. Without a doubt, money affects people, so the Bible talks at length on the subject of money. God, through the words of the Bible, speaks about our need of money and how we can use money—and abuse it. How money can bless a life, or lead to its ruin.

So don't be shy! You can—and should—talk about money. God is interested in your thoughts about it, your relationship to it, and the value you place on it. He knows you need it for your well-being, and He has some good ideas on how to manage it so it doesn't give you heartburn.

As for the chili pepper—perhaps there's something in your medicine cabinet for that!

The Impact of Influence

Nothing is so infectious as example.
François de La Rochefoucauld

Marnie threw her hands in the air. "You simply won't listen to me!" she cried in exasperation during a visit with her aging mother. Marnie believed she was seeing disturbing signs of distraction and forgetfulness in her mother's conversations, but her mother refused to discuss the matter. With a sinking heart, the distraught daughter left her mother's house once again, realizing she had no control over her mother's attitude.

As you watch your loved ones making ill-considered choices, of course you're frustrated when they won't listen to reason. You've tried intervention, but they've only dug in their heels. Despite your pleas, prayers, and appeals, you can't change the direction they're intent on going. Finally, you're forced to admit that, for better or for worse, they have the right to make their own decisions.

But you do have influence, and influence has impact. The things you do and say can either deepen the chasm or build a bridge—a bridge they may use to renew their relationship with you. Your example can either shut down the possibility of further communication or encourage more discussion when everyone's had a chance to cool off.

Try as we might, not one of us has the ability to control another person—child, spouse, friend, parent, co-worker, neighbor. God doesn't choose to control people, either. Instead, He reaches out to persuade us through the words of Scripture and His work in our hearts. He is our perfect example of how to influence others!

A Matter of Belief

A man's most valuable trait
is a judicious sense of what not to believe.
Euripides

What we believe matters. Our deeply held beliefs make the difference between discontent and satisfaction, unkindness and gentleness, coldness and compassion, frustration and fulfillment, lonely days and a happy life.

The person who believes that no one cares about her will find in every real or imagined slight further confirmation of her original belief. One who believes she's no good at anything will start any project expecting to fail, and the first fumble will convince her she's right—she's no good at anything. And the young woman who believes that the world is her adversary will find nothing less than a very formidable foe as she gets out into the world.

What you believe matters, including what you believe about God. Believe He is what He says He is—compassionate, kind, loving, and forgiving—and you will find Him all those things, and more. Believe He is with you always and desires the best for you, and you will discover Him with you today, tomorrow, and forever. He is your strength when you need it, rest when you reach out for it, and comfort to take you through the changes and chances of life.

How you see the world, how you treat people, and even how you treat yourself depends on what you believe. Have you thought through your beliefs lately, and have you examined them? How are they working for you? Yes, your beliefs are important. Test everything.

Which Way?

Self-knowledge is the beginning of self-improvement.

Proverb

There are two kinds of people in the world: those who ponder projects for so long that they never get started. They're the procrastinators. And then there are the people who dive in head first, only to realize the water is deeper and rougher than they had thought—but it's too late now! They're the impulsive ones. Where do you fit in?

Maybe we lean one way or the other, but most of us can claim membership in both groups. We know what it's like to put things off and what it's like to act on impulse. When delay causes a lost opportunity, we wish we had acted sooner. But then what about the time delay that kept us from grabbing something that sounded too good to be true—and was?

When impulsive risk-taking results in consequences we could have avoided, we regret we didn't give the matter a little more time and thought. Yet again, most of us can recall a time our quick wit brought us the thrill of having risked—and won.

Procrastination control? We need it! We have to make a move if we expect to go anywhere. Impulse control? We need it! What we want right now might not be what we want for the long term.

For procrastinators, for impulsive sorts—for us—God's guidance helps us get going when we need to, and hold back when caution is the wisest way. And the best news is this: He's there to lift us up and dust us off when we just don't get it right.

Please, Please Yourself

No one can make you feel inferior without your consent.
Eleanor Roosevelt

You're not going to please everyone. You're bound to ruffle a few feathers, say, when you assert yourself and claim what is rightfully yours…step forward as a contender willing to compete for the prize… insist on being heard and respected in your family, among your friends, and in your community.

But some of us don't dare, because displeased people are likely to push back, especially at first. So we're left with two options. One, we can retreat and settle back into the role that's more comfortable for us—and them. In short, we can allow others to decide who we are and what we'll do. Or two, we can push forward. Call it tough love, maybe. We assure those around us through our words and actions that we respect them and care for them, but at the same time, we respect and care for ourselves, too. They matter, and so do we.

God created you to live a life fully and uniquely yours, but you aren't able unless you take control of your feelings about yourself. After all, you can't expect someone else to value you if *you* don't value you! And every person God put in the world has value—immense value. Including you.

Love yourself, because God does. What difference does this thought make in the way you see yourself? How might you act differently around others? How willing are you to ruffle a few feathers?

Unchangeable God

Progress is impossible without change;
and those who cannot change their minds
cannot change anything.

George Bernard Shaw

The longer we live, the more we know that things change, people change, and we change. Yet change, even desired change, causes anxiety! Some psychologists have suggested that welcome life events like marriage, the birth of a baby, and a new home can bring on as much stress as unwelcome events, such as divorce, job loss, or natural catastrophe.

It's unwelcome, unforeseen, and unexpected changes that make us feel completely out of control. And in truth, these events *are* out of our control. What's left for us to decide is how we're going to respond, because continuing as we were before is either not possible or no longer realistic. The only choice that puts us in a place where we can start managing unwelcome change is humble acceptance. Humble acceptance lets us take control of what remains under our control—most importantly, our attitude. Will we accept, or will we not?

In so many cases, our unwelcome change is simply God's amazing hand at work in our lives. Stress-producing? Right now, yes! That's why God, who controls all change, Himself never changes. You can rely on Him with the same unquestioning trust that a small child puts in her loving parent's wisdom, strength, and love. The more things change in your life, the more He stays the same—today, tomorrow, forever.

First Choice

The strongest principle of growth lies in human choice.

George Eliot

When the choice lies between something you do want and something you don't want, you have it easy! But many choices aren't as clear cut. Whichever way you choose has its pros and cons. For example: you're offered a promotion with your company, but to take it you would need to move away from a house you love and a city where you're known and established. Or suppose you would like your elderly parent to move in with you so you could see to their safety and well-being, but you're concerned about the impact on your privacy and time with your family.

Choices are blessings, because when we have choices, we have control over certain aspects of our lives. At the same time, choices distress us if we just don't know what to choose! We want to do the right thing, but undesirable consequences could materialize. Are we prepared to face them? Of course a promotion sounds attractive, but leaving a familiar place and longtime friends doesn't. Yes, you want to take care of your parents, but you also need time for yourself, your spouse and kids.

Many times in life, you face tough choices, the kind God is capable of helping you sort out. Just ask Him. He can lead you to the best choice, and when He does, He will give you strength to handle the whole choice—its pros and its cons. Before you choose anything, choose Him.

A Heap of Trouble

Call upon me in the day of trouble:
I will deliver thee.

Psalm 50:15

We know what it feels like when troubles pile up, one after the other. And they invariably do! When money is tight, that's when the dog gets sick, the refrigerator conks out, the car won't start, and the utility bills skyrocket. When we're not feeling our best, that's when the kids bring their friends home for dinner, the boss wants a report ASAP, and we have tickets to a long-awaited concert this evening.

Though there's little we can do to prevent troubles from coming at us from all directions at the worst possible moment, there are a few things we can remember to lighten the burden. First, it's temporary! One by one, we'll fix what needs fixing, solve what needs solving, and find the resources to do it. Perhaps we'll need a little help from our friends—just ask.

Second, life goes on. The kids have to eat a make-do meal? Your report is a day late this once? You opt to pass the tickets on to someone else? It's okay.

Third—and most important: When troubles pile up, there's no better time than now to remember how big, how high, how all-encompassing God's love is for you. No, He may not choose to miraculously sweep away all that's bothering you in an instant, but He always chooses to care about you and what you're going through. With Him at your side, you can get through a heap of troubles—His promise! Give Him a call.

Friends Help

I always felt that the great high privilege,
relief, and comfort of friendship
was that one had to explain nothing.

Katherine Mansfield

Imagine sitting down with someone who always knows when you're tired, frustrated, or depressed. "Easy!" you might say, "because I would look tired, frustrated, or depressed!" But now imagine this person realizes that you don't want to talk about it. So no questions asked; just a quiet, gentle presence…along with a steaming hot mug of cocoa.

If such a person is in your life, you have a true friend. That's the one you can depend on to be there and support you, but who never tries to manage your problems for you. With or without words, she understands you, and in the same way, you understand her. With no explanations necessary, if it's important to you, it's important to her.

God is that kind of friend, and more. You may not know the words to say, or even be ready to say them, but He hears you. He sees the anguish of your heart, the feelings too hard to express, the painful memories you have never shared with anyone. You may not be able to explain the reason for your feelings, but He understands. Just sitting in His presence is all the conversation you need for renewal, refreshment, and heart-deep rest. You have a friend in Him.

Trying Times

Bad times have a scientific value.
These are occasions a good learner would not miss.
Ralph Waldo Emerson

Few of us jump at the chance to take an exam, whether it's to pass a class, become certified, or get a driver's license. But after the ordeal is over and we've passed with flying colors (or at least passed!), we feel good—and proud, too. We've proven to ourselves that we can do it.

Trying times work in a similar way. While few of us welcome them and we don't like going through them, they reveal our capability, strength, and know-how in a way nothing else can. Working through a problem applies our thinking skills, and asking others for help with our problems builds relationships. Adversity tests our patience and resolve, and adds to our maturity and life experience. In addition, adversity instills empathy for others facing hardship. Only by going through it ourselves can we fully appreciate how it feels. We've taken the exam. We've been there and done that. We can look back and feel proud that we came through it.

Like a caring teacher, God permits tests in life's classroom. It's not because He wants to know whether or not you can pass, because He already knows. He knows how much grit, strength, and resilience you possess. He knows what you can do, and now He wants you to know it, too.

Nurture Your Heart

Patience is bitter, but its fruit is sweet.

Proverb

"You just have to wait!" the veteran gardener laughed. The young couple surveyed their plot of tilled soil and rows of newly planted seedlings. They looked doubtful. "Plants need time," he said. "Nurture them, keep the weeds away, and you'll have a good crop all summer long."

We're not unlike the young couple when we're impatient for answers, for solutions, for normalcy to return to a life plowed up by misfortune. But rarely do we immediately get what we want. Instead, we have to "plant seeds" by getting practical advice, putting feasible plans in place, and making sound decisions. Then we need to wait for these seeds to grow and blossom—for our actions to prove successful and for needed change to take effect. As with a garden, it takes time. It takes patience.

By planting good seeds now—love, kindness, compassion, faith in God, a healthy lifestyle, a joyful attitude—you can look forward to a "garden" of strength, confidence, resilience, and serenity. As you pull out the "weeds" of anxiety and discouragement, you'll start gaining control over situations that frustrate you now. Be patient! Nurture your heart and soul with God-given hope and confidence. At the right time, you will see and enjoy the many fruits of your effort.

When It's Unexpected

God gives us always strength enough, and sense enough, for everything He wants us to do.

John Ruskin

Who would have expected it? You take a seasonal job to earn a little extra money, and it becomes the start of a fulfilling, decades-long career. You agree to go with a friend to a basketball game, and you end up an avid fan. You happen to meet an old classmate, and romance blooms.

Of course, not all unforeseen developments are as sweet. There are those complications we never imagined and aren't prepared to handle. There are unanticipated delays, glitches, malfunctions, difficulties, and cost overruns. Sometimes we thoroughly expect to succeed, but for any number of reasons, we don't. We believe we have every chance of getting to our goal, but things don't turn out and we fall far short.

And how about these unexpected events—ones God designs especially for you. When they happen, some might seem less than promising, but in the end, you wouldn't have chosen it any other way. A heartbreaking disappointment leads to a much better opportunity down the road. An alarming reversal in your life's direction puts you on the path to greater fulfillment and satisfaction. A painful parting opens the door to a bright new beginning.

Expect the unexpected! From happy developments to challenging changes that come to you from out of the blue, there's a heavenly hand at the controls. That you can always expect!

Talk, Talk, Talk

Do not let any unwholesome talk come out of your mouths, but only what is helpful for building others up according to their needs, that it may benefit those who listen.
Ephesians 4:29 NIV

A snarky comment, yes, but it was meant for her ears only. We had a good laugh! Then she forgot it was confidential, and she repeated it—and you know what happened then. Those few carelessly spoken words set off a maelstrom of anger, hurt, and misunderstanding.

Talking is easy, but controlling where our words go is impossible. Controlling what comes out of our mouths, however, isn't impossible. Not always easy, but not impossible, and God tells us how to go about it. He tells us how to take control of what we say, because once the words leave our lips, there's no taking them back.

The Bible urges us to speak as gently and as affirmatively as the truth allows. We're counseled to use words that build up instead of tear down—words that promote peace and harmony rather than sow conflict and discontent. We're to speak words of hope and encouragement, gratitude and praise.

The words that come out of our mouths, however, don't begin at our lips, but in our minds and hearts. Where there are no unkind thoughts, unkind words never have a chance to form. Where there's a heart full of love, there's no room for speech full of malice.

Kind thoughts, loving heart—now there's word-control that really works!

Minding the Moments

This is the day which the LORD hath made;
we will rejoice and be glad in it.

Psalm 118:24

After a hectic day at work, Shelley pulls into her driveway. At the sound of her schnauzer's bark behind the kitchen door, she smiles. The anticipation of homemade soup, simmering in the slow cooker, makes her eager to sit down and enjoy a leisurely meal. Home! Then it hits her. She doesn't remember crossing a major intersection, getting on the highway, or passing through a nearby shopping district. She recalls nothing of the drive home!

At one time or another, most of us have had an experience like Shelley's. We're on autopilot. We're going through the motions, but our attention lies a thousand miles away. Instead of thinking about what we're doing right now, we're planning what we're going to do next…fretting about yesterday…worrying about tomorrow…solving imaginary problems. On autopilot, we're filling our minds with what we have no power to control instead of what we have control over—this moment.

Attentiveness to the moment brings blessings, and here are three of them:

- Freedom from worry about the past and the future. One is gone, the other yet to come—but this moment is here for you to use to its fullest.
- Satisfaction with what you're doing right now. You may discover real enjoyment, see things you've never noticed before, find better ways of doing things.
- Memory of having done it!

The Life of a Complaint

It's better to light a candle than curse the darkness.

Proverb

Complaints don't walk, they run—and they rarely ever travel alone! It takes only one grumpy person in a slow-moving line to start griping about the wait, and pretty soon the whole line begins to rumble with grumbles. Or perhaps you've had this experience—you wake up feeling a little grouchy, and the first thing you do is fire off a complaint. Then, all day long, nothing goes right, and it's complain, complain, complain! Things to complain about jump out at you from all directions!

Yes, some things can really annoy us—and it seems that the longer we live, the longer the list! But complaining about them does us no favor. Complaints accentuate our powerlessness in the face of situations we can't control (such as that slow-moving line). Frustration increases and anger takes root. Complaints amplify what's wrong—or what we think is wrong—and leave us in no mood to figure out how to make it right (or at least ignore it).

When you feel complaints coming on, stand aside. Let them pass right on through. If they venture into your thinking or step into your attitude, block the road. Life is a much more pleasant journey for you and for everyone else around you without the company of complaints!

Prayer Gets Rid of Worry

Let not your heart be troubled, neither let it be afraid.

John 14:27

Why worry? That's an easy question. Worry comes naturally to all of us. We want to pay our bills on time, but how can we when the money won't stretch that far? We long for good health, but can we really expect it after these test results? We thought we had the kids' after-school activities completely taken care of, and at the last minute, the arrangements fell apart—so now what? Yet worry leads to more worry, until we're worried about our sanity (another worry). That's why worry is never an answer—it's a question.

What are you worried about? What is the fear you're facing, the blow that blindsided you, the heavy load you just can't get off of your shoulders? You know what it is, because you've been worried about it. It's what has been keeping you up at night and giving you fits all day. Small and insignificant, or major and life-altering—either way, you're worried.

Now take the matter to God in prayer. Tell Him about it, and then listen for His answer. Let Him lift your worries from your heart and mind. Let Him replace your anxiety with His wisdom, your unease with His peace. Let Him answer you with the comfort of His presence and the warmth of His love.

Ask Him about what worries you. God has the answer, because He *is* the answer.

God-Blessed Freedom

No man is free who is not master of himself.

Epictetus

Freedom and limits don't go together, because limits take away freedom, right? At least that's the way our minds work, but not God's. He takes the opposite view—God-blessed freedom is possible only when we're willing to follow God-placed limits.

It's not hard to understand how it works. When we submit to God-placed limits on our thoughts—such as no malice, no meanness, no indecency—we avoid falling into negative, harmful, and destructive mindsets. His thought-limits free us to focus on the positive aspects of life, appreciate the blessings we possess, love being who we are, and experience genuine joy.

When we accept God-placed limits on our actions, we avoid setting out on dangerous paths—paths that lead to disappointment, despair, and hopelessness. Only then are we free to take the God-blessed path He has in mind for us, the path that leads to stability, confidence, and fulfillment. When we obey God-placed limits on the words we speak, we never need to tell a lie to cover a lie, or blush with shame when our words come back to us. Our words encourage, inspire, lift up, freeing others from the burdens that keep them down.

God-blessed freedom includes being able to ask forgiveness when we step over God-placed limits—and we do. He invites us to come to Him, and He will strengthen us, refresh us, and renew our freedom in Him. To His love and compassion for us, there are no limits!

First Things First

I have been driven many times to my knees
by the overwhelming conviction that I had nowhere else to go.

Abraham Lincoln

Last resort...pray! But why wait until all else has failed?

Perhaps because we prefer to work things out for ourselves. We sweat, strain, and struggle, and breathe a sigh of relief when we finally make it through. Maybe we offer God a slight nod of gratitude, but maybe not. We did it ourselves, learned a lot, and we'll do better next time. We feel pretty powerful!

Next time, though, things get more complicated. Isn't that just like life? The problem involves more people...more time...more money... more stress than we're used to. And it's not just one problem this time, but several. All the sweat, strain, struggle in the world isn't going to get us through this one—we're just not powerful enough! Is now the time to pray? Yes. And we can just imagine God saying with a laugh, "What took you so long?"

Prayer is not an excuse to sit back and do nothing, because God has never promised to do for us what we can do for ourselves. What He has promised, however, is to hear our prayer and give us what we need to handle whatever challenges we're facing.

Why put prayer at the end of the list? When it's right up there at the top, you know how to put first things first!

Beyond Appearances

How little do they see what is,
who frame their hasty judgments upon that which seems.
Robert Southey

It turns out that the manager with the messiest desk can locate a file in the blink of an eye. The professor with the unruly hair and mismatched socks lectures with meticulous care and exactitude. The couple with the smallest, most modest home in the neighborhood holds the biggest bank account. You can think of many more examples from your own experience. Things aren't always what they seem!

From the outside, your days might look chaotic. Yesterday's urgency is now second to today's rush job, and new problems are popping up by the hour. You hurry from one place to the next with no time to catch your breath in between.

But underneath the apparent hubbub, there's deep meaning—do you see it? You're involved with people…you're helping, caring, encouraging, and championing others. You're engaged in productive activities, you have fulfilling responsibilities, and you find ways to express yourself and add beauty to the world. If you look beneath it all, you will see what God sees.

What's really important isn't all the to-do's that are (or aren't) getting done today. What ultimately matters isn't what's happening on the outside, but what's happening in you. You're out there. You're doing. You're making a difference. And you're looking great!

Giving Is Receiving

So in everything, do to others
what you would have them do to you.
Matthew 7:12 NIV

You probably know someone who simply irks you. It could be for any number of reasons—constant chatter, negative or judgmental attitude, privacy-piercing questions. Whatever it is, it's so irritating!

In all likelihood, the people we find hard to like don't realize how they come across to others. It's possible that the chatterbox feels she's being upbeat and sociable...the self-appointed judge believes she's standing up for her rightful opinions...the invasive inquirer has convinced herself that she's doing well by showing concern for other people. Informing them otherwise is what we might yearn to do, but an anger-ridden, ugly-truth-telling session rarely achieves desired change (and might turn an irksome person into an enemy!). These people probably have taken their share of rebuffs, so why add offense to offense? What's more apt to achieve positive change is a kindly response.

We can take control of the conversation by offering not what we've received, but what we'd like to receive. Warmth, tolerance, and gentleness send a powerful message, too! By our example, we're showing them what genuine friendliness looks like...what thoughtful opinions sound like... what respectful sharing feels like.

Try it, and who knows? It could be the start of a wonderful friendship!

What Really Matters

Many men go fishing all of their lives
without knowing that it is not fish they are after.
Henry David Thoreau

Have you ever stopped to think about what really matters to you—you alone? No one's looking over your shoulder. There's no one you need to impress or prove yourself to; there's no one expecting you to fill a certain role, and no one to judge you if you don't reach a particular goal or milestone. If this were all true, would your priorities change? Would the way you spend your money, time, and energy shift in other directions?

If your answer is "yes," then it's possible you're doing many things you really don't want to do, or you see no reason to do. Deep down inside, you resent the time and effort you're pouring into these activities, because they matter more to others than they do to you. In short, your heart just isn't in it.

Unfortunately, some of the activities that come to our minds could be necessities! Then it helps to remind ourselves why we're doing what we're doing—it's to earn money so we can buy food for the family or save up for a great vacation, or to keep a pleasant and comfortable home, or to regain our health and wellbeing. We're taking control. We're spending our time in a constructive way, and we have a real purpose.

A non-necessity, however, can be delegated to the person who thinks it's really important…cut back so we don't spend so much energy on it… or eliminated altogether!

A Little Nudge

Nothing is too difficult–you only need to know how.
Proverb

Visiting a friend, Jen noticed the photos of delicious-looking salads and shiny, ripe fruits that dotted her refrigerator door. "So what's this?" Jen asked. "That's my reminder board," her friend replied. "Whenever I'm tempted to get a bag of chips or a box of cookies, I look at all these pictures. It works! I remember that my goal this year is to eat healthier, and so I grab an apple or a handful of carrot sticks!"

At the time, Jen was worried about her stress level. She noticed that even small, minor inconveniences made her short-tempered and brought on a painful tension headache. "I've got to control my stress level!" she resolved to herself. So she took a hint from her friend's refrigerator door.

When she got home, Jen looked up a few short quotes—words reminding her to breathe deeply, keep things in perspective, remember God's presence in her life, and smile. She clipped a couple inspiring photos from a magazine—a lily floating on a sheltered pond…a bird resting in the branches of a shady tree…the sun's rays spreading across the ripples of a tranquil sea. She made her own reminder board. It helped her de-stress. It helped her control her emotions before they took control of her.

Would daily reminders help you regain control? What else might work for you? Sometimes a little nudge in the right direction is all it takes!

A Limited Budget

What had seemed easy in imagination was rather hard in reality.

Lucy Maud Montgomery

Anyone who has ever been on, and stuck to, a budget has learned how to buy carefully. With only a limited amount of money to spend, the shopper selects the best price, or, in some cases, foregoes the purchase altogether. Her budget tells her that she just can't afford it right now.

In much the same way, God has given each of us the same budget of time (24 hours per day), along with a personal, individual budget of strength and energy. Not one of us can boast all the time in the world, all the strength in the world, and all the energy in the world! We can afford only a certain number of tasks, projects, and responsibilities today without going beyond our budget. When we overspend? Then time's too short to do everything we've taken on. We lose control.

The same thing with our strength and energy budgets. Though some of us are stronger than others and some of us are more energetic than others, each of us has a limit. Go beyond it? We're in trouble. We're tired, tense, and often succumb to despair.

Buy carefully! Before you reach for the next activity, hobby, responsibility, or product, consider your budget. Do you have the time to spend? Strength to accommodate it? Energy to see it through? Perhaps there's a better alternative. Or maybe, as appealing as it is, it just doesn't fit into your budget right now.

Directional Signs

I sought the LORD, and he heard me,
and delivered me from all my fears.
Psalm 34:4

That red light at the intersection tells you to stop, doesn't it? How about the No Entry sign next to the freeway off-ramp? Tells you not to head up that direction. You see the signs, note what they're saying, but you don't stop and stare at them. Instead, you take in what they're telling you to do—or not do—and move accordingly.

The feeling of being out of control is a sign, too. It tells us that something isn't going right, but all too often we stop right there and stare at the sign. The more we stare, the more emotionally out of control we feel. The more out of control we feel, the less we're able to take the steps that would help us regain control!

The next time you feel out of control, see it as a sign. Read it, and then let your focus shift from the sign itself to what the sign could be telling you. Things like:

- You could never handle this alone, and you were never meant to.
- Every burden is made lighter by sharing it with someone who cares.
- Help is available. Think about it. Pray about it. There is a way!

You see the sign. It's in the stress you've been under for weeks (years?). It's in the words of despair, spoken or unspoken. It's in the feeling that nothing is going quite right. Make a U-turn and go to God, and get back on track with peace of mind and heart.

Bully Behavior

I can do all things through Christ which strengtheneth me.

Philippians 4:13

Bullies aren't confined to the schoolyard. Bullies show up in homes and workplaces, churches, organizations, and community centers—in short, wherever people gather. You might not recognize them at first, because they're not hurling childish insults at you, daring you to jump off the top of the swing set, or threatening to tell the teacher on you. No, they've long ago graduated to more sophisticated forms of harassment.

They exert power over us through subtle and not-so-subtle intimidation—teasing (can't you take a joke?) or browbeating (listen to me!) or belittling (if you were smarter, you would understand what I'm saying). Like the timid kindergartener facing an ill-tempered ten-year-old, we feel small, scared, and helpless—even if we're careful not to let them know. We naturally retreat from them whenever possible, hoping to protect ourselves from harm.

Is there an adult-sized bully in your life? Pray for that person, because he or she needs your prayers. Most bullies, you know, feel insecure. Their behavior is their method of controlling others. Pray, then think of ways—even small ways—you can, with love and gentleness, assert yourself in their presence. Remove control from them to you. And most important of all, remember this: both of you are deeply loved by your heavenly Father.

Comfortable Ambiguity

Certitude is not the test of certainty.
We have been cocksure of many things that were not so.
Oliver Wendell Holmes, Jr.

Clear as glass! At least, clear as glass that's been scrubbed sparkly clean, preferably by someone else! Unfortunately, life situations aren't always as clear as a freshly wiped window. Sometimes the facts lie hidden under layers of rumor, speculation, and misinformation. We can't see anything with clarity or know anything for sure.

Most of us find ambiguity unsettling. We don't like being unsure of the facts, not knowing who's telling the truth and who isn't…what really happened and what didn't…how to react and how not to react. In a rush to gain control, we'll often take only what makes sense to us and fits in with what we already know or believe to be true. Yet there's a risk, because we may not have picked the facts.

In many cases, a little detective work on our part rubs away some of the uncertainties and reveals a clearer, larger picture. But in others, no amount of wiping (or wishing) will uncover all the details, all the essentials, everything we'd like to know. We just have to get comfortable with ambiguity, at least for the time being.

In spiritual life, too, God invites you to get comfortable with ambiguity. His plans and His ways are rarely clear as glass to you. Why does a certain situation exist in your life? Why aren't all your questions answered? You can't see it now, but there's a reason. When the time comes, He will make it crystal clear, and you will be amazed at the wisdom of His ways.

An Old-Fashioned Value

You can't know too much, but you can say too much.

Calvin Coolidge

Calvin Coolidge, the 30th president of the United States, is remembered as a man of few words. Though he occupied the White House in the 1920s—a loud, raucous, and rowdy era—he held to the old-fashioned virtue of verbal restraint.

Today, we're living in an era of free, uninhibited expression and turbulent, often unsettling, change. What's more, social media gives all of us a public place to vent and whine, confess and criticize, blame and complain, and make our opinions known. Declaration, not restraint, is the order of the day!

Yet the wisest among us still practice restraint in what we say and how we say it. It's a time-honored way to protect privacy and maintain a good reputation. Restraint teaches us to control our temper so we don't lash out in anger, to keep confidences so we don't betray others, and to know what we're saying before we speak so we don't pass along half-truths or misinformation.

One place where you never have to worry about saying too much, however, is when you're deep in prayer with God. If it's on your mind, in your heart, at the tip of your tongue, you can tell Him. Then listen as He helps you get it all sorted out.

Pushing the Right Buttons

It takes two flints to make a fire.

Louisa May Alcott

The people who know you best are the ones who can really push your buttons. A certain word, phrase, or look on their part is all it takes to kick-start feelings of fear, anger, or even rage. You're not alone, because we've all been there. And if we're honest, we must admit that we've pushed a few buttons ourselves upon occasion.

Other people are able to control our emotions when we have handed over control to them. Either consciously or unconsciously, we've placed in someone else's power our emotional well-being, our peace of mind, and our ability to choose our own responses. We get mad at ourselves, because we don't like feeling manipulated; and we're bound to resent the person who's able to affect us at such a deep and personal level.

Emotions are blessings from God, and they enable you to experience life to the fullest. But yours are yours, and no one else's! So maybe it's time to disarm some of the "buttons." Think about the situations where your emotions are likely to get out of control, and ask yourself why this is happening. Chances are there's more than meets the eye! Then take responsibility for feeling the way you do. Plan a clear-headed, rational response. Rehearse it in your mind. Next time someone pushes your buttons, you control the outcome!

The Power of Lasting Love

I have loved thee with an everlasting love.

Jeremiah 31:3

Success or wealth, talent or fame, introvert or extrovert has nothing to do with it. Almost all of us can admit that, at some point in life, we have felt lonely, dejected, or unloved. And for some, feelings of unworthiness, of unlovability, cast a dark cloud of doubt over every justly deserved compliment, well-earned achievement, and potentially fulfilling relationship.

God has woven a thread of love throughout the Bible because He wants us to not only believe in, but experience, genuine love. He reveals His love for us in how He treated His biblical people. Despite the many times they let Him down, He lifted them up. No matter how dejected they felt or how foolishly they acted, He responded with compassion, forgiveness, and love. Though often they left Him to find spiritual satisfaction in earthly pursuits, He always remained present for them. His love stayed strong.

Today, God loves you with the same ardent, resilient, and ever-present love. It's His love that can dispel your feelings of unworthiness and provide lasting confidence and healthy self-esteem. It's His love that convinces you to love yourself, no matter who you are, and compels you to love others—no matter who they are. It's His love that creates love, and more love!

A Light Take

Proud people breed sad sorrows for themselves.

Emily Brontë

"Take your work seriously, but not yourself," the cautionary adage goes. It's good advice for the workplace, and also for life. "Take your life seriously," we might say, "but with yourself? Go lightly!"

Our life is serious business, because God has put us here for a purpose. He gave us our bodies, minds, and all our senses so we could enjoy the world and the blessings that surround us—the splendor of a sun-kissed ocean…the sweep of an open prairie…the aroma of baking bread…the squeeze of a loved one's hand. Our lives are enriched by the ability to bring help, comfort, and compassion to the people we meet…to share our time, energy, and resources with others…to receive joy and satisfaction in using the skills and talents He has given us. A joyful, fulfilling life is ours when we take seriously God's reason for giving us life.

But when we take ourselves seriously, we're in for a bumpy ride. Self-interest leads to greed, and arrogance convinces us that we can do no wrong. Unhealthy pride won't stand for constructive criticism, and a big ego invites an even bigger fall. Conceit leads us to think we've got to be in control at all times, and we know how realistic that is!

So smile at yourself today. Treat yourself lightly. Forgive your faults and laugh at your idiosyncrasies. You can do it, because God is very serious about His love for you.

Depend on God

How little security have we
when we trust our happiness in the hands of others.
William Hazlitt

It's an all-too-common story. A young girl lacking in self-confidence looks for someone to provide it. She gravitates toward the first boy who floods her with attention and tells her the things she longs to hear. Soon she's completely dependent on an undependable person for the confidence she craves, her boyfriend the judge of her worth.

It's not just young people, however, who depend on other people—or other things—for their sense of worth. Adults, both men and women, sometimes rely on their spouse, friends, or associates for a positive self-image. They might look to money, possessions, or a job title to make them feel good about themselves. They're hanging onto people and things they can't control to provide their inmost needs. This, too, is an all-too-common story.

Unhealthy dependencies are far from what God intends for you. That's why He invites you to trust in and depend on Him for your heart-deep desires. He knows you need confidence, and He gives it by walking beside you. He knows you need fulfillment, and He provides it by giving you interests and responsibilities, passions and purpose. He knows you need security, and He delivers it by assuring you of His presence. He knows you need love, and He gives it—a love you can depend on.

Lean on Him alone. It's a happy and wonderful story!

Healthy Reliance

No member of a crew is praised
for the rugged individuality of his rowing.

Ralph Waldo Emerson

In old westerns, the hero single-handedly saves the day, and then he rides off into the sunset. While we realize the story is a fictional one, many of us have taken the lone hero as our ideal. If we've got a problem, we want to solve it by ourselves, our way. No outsiders needed!

But reality is this: We live in an interdependent world. We rely on one another, even people we may not know personally, like the state trooper who keeps our roadways safe…the trucker who delivers food to the supermarket…the airline pilot who gets us to our destination. No one person can do it all.

Closer to home, too, interdependence is vital. Without friends and family to listen, care, and support us, the fears and frustrations of daily life get out of control. Easily solvable problems become huge difficulties when we refuse to reach out for help. We begin to imagine it's us against the world—but it isn't, and it never is. God has put us in this world together with the intention that we live together in mutual love and compassion, offering support and service to one another.

Who are the people in your support system? How comfortable do you feel reaching out to them when you're feeling overwhelmed with worry or stress? Don't go it alone! Strength for the challenges of life rests in the strength of all of us working together.

A New Approach

Behold, I make all things new.
Revelation 21:5

If you spent any time at the beach as a child, it's likely you've built a few sand castles back in the day. Whether it was a simple mound or an elaborate fortress with pointed roofs and rounded turrets, you regarded your work with pride and satisfaction—but then the tide rolled in and washed it all away! Next time, you promised yourself, you'd build further back from the shore. You learned your lesson.

As adults, we don't always learn so quickly from our mistakes and miscalculations. We have a tendency to point the finger at uncontrollable forces to explain why things don't work out for us, or a particular plan of ours isn't bringing about the changes we're looking for. Sure, sometimes forces beyond our control will thwart our plans, and there's nothing we can do, or could have done, to change the outcome. But other times, it's us. We're not willing to learn from what goes wrong and make corrections.

Before you give up on that diet...that savings plan...that dream you've held in your heart for so long, remember what it was like to watch the tide flood your sand creation. You didn't give up building sand castles because you couldn't control the sea, did you? No, because stacking sand was too much fun! So next time, you adjusted. You did what you set out to do, but you did it a little differently.

Need inspiration? Ask God—He's good at new creations!

Step by Step

If you only keep adding little by little,
it will soon become a big heap.

Hesiod

After a weekend of filling cracks and sanding walls in their older home, Jill and David looked around in dismay. Dust had settled everywhere! Every table, chair, and shelf was coated with a thick layer of grit. The floors were caked with grime, and even the afternoon sunbeams that made it through the filmy windows were teeming with swirling particles of light, powdery dust. There was so much to clean up that the couple had no idea where to start.

Whenever the task is daunting, discouragement sets in. Where to start? How to start? Yet there are few big to-dos that can't be broken down into small ones—and accomplished. There aren't many out-of-control jobs that won't yield to our taking control of some small part. Results won't come right away, but come they do as we keep moving forward, inch by inch. For Jill and David, it was room by room. Yes, it took a month of Sundays, they laughed later, but eventually their dust-free home sparkled!

Whether you're struggling with an overpowering emotion or a colossal project, step-by-step lets you get it under your control. With each small success, celebrate your work. Then, even if it takes a month of Sundays, you'll find yourself standing right where you want to be!

And with each step, take God along with you. There's power in His presence, strength in His help, and patience—always patience, no matter how long the journey.

Soul Food

We are not human beings having a spiritual experience.
We are spiritual beings having a human experience.
Teilhard de Chardin

How long has it been since you've had a serious conversation about matters of the spirit?

For most of us, it's been a long time. Maybe never. While we may easily chat about the latest celebrity doings, we're cautious when it comes to spiritual matters. Perhaps we don't want to offend a friend or family member who may not share our views. Perhaps we don't want to come across as overly serious or sentimental. But again, perhaps there's a deeper reason—we're not sure what we believe when it comes to spiritual things.

We're more than a body—much, much more! But what is this "more" that can perceive transcendence in nature, act with sacrificial love toward others, and sense the unseen presence of a divine power? These are only a few of the ways God reaches out to us. He regularly feeds us and nourishes us, inviting us to experience His "more" within our everyday lives. He gives us soul food!

You aren't able to control the spiritual experiences God gives to you, but you are able to welcome Him with daily quiet time for spiritual thinking…attentiveness to spiritual things…and conversations about spiritual matters with those closest to you. Share your soul food with others. It's how to taste what God has done in your life and savor what you believe about spiritual things.

Care Without Controlling

Learn to do thy part and leave the rest to heaven.
John Henry Newman

When the life of someone we love spirals out of control, so does ours. We wonder what we could have said or done differently to keep them from taking such a risky, foolhardy course of action. Somehow we feel responsible for the decisions they're making. Conversations we've had with them play over and over in our minds, and we wonder what we can do now to protect them from the heartbreak that most certainly lies ahead.

We care deeply about them, and that's why our feelings are so powerful. Yet sometimes the best and most positive kind of caring comes not by holding tight, but by opening our arms, letting go, and waiting for our loved one's return. God does that all the time. No matter how far away we may stray, or how long it's been since we've even thought about asking for His help, He's there for us when we're ready to return to Him. Why? Because He loves us, and because of His love for us, He cares—cares deeply.

God cares so much about you that He refuses to control you. Though He invites you to follow in His way and will give you the strength to do so, He never forces you to accept what you don't want to accept. You are you—and God is God—God who promises to be there with open arms, waiting for the return of all His loved ones, wherever they have been.

Precious Life

To everything there is a season,
and a time to every purpose under the heaven.
Ecclesiastes 3:1

Most of us don't grasp how precious life is until we lose someone close to us. Suddenly, a familiar voice is silent, a beloved face is gone, a comforting presence is no longer there. With painful loss comes a deepened awareness that each of us rests in God's caring hands.

We can beg Him to tell us why this heartbreak, and we can express rage against Him for this blow to our happiness. In fact, bold, vigorous, courageous prayer is the kind He very likely welcomes from us in our times of sorrow! Passionate prayer puts us squarely in His presence, honestly articulates the depth of our feelings, and then, when all our words are spent, leaves us in a place where we're ready to listen.

When your prayers come from deep within your heart and soul, how does He answer? Perhaps the warmth of His presence to fill the emptiness of your heart…the assurance of your loved one's peace…words of Scripture to remind you of His many promises… an awareness that life is not to be taken for granted, but lived fully and joyfully…a new appreciation for the people in your life today.

With God comes the inexpressible knowledge that, no matter how hard it is now, He hears…and understands.

Giving Control

Whoever sows generously will also reap generously.
2 Corinthians 9:6 NIV

Scott, a busy executive, spends every Thursday evening volunteering at a youth counseling center. Asked why he devotes so many hours to at-risk teens, he says, "Because I was born into a family able to give me an opportunity to succeed, and now I want to share it with those who were not as blessed as I have been."

God has blessed each of us with something to share with others. It might be a skill or talent we possess that would enrich the lives of others, if only we were there to teach them. It might be our gift of attentive listening that could lift the burden of loneliness from the hearts of others, or our gift of speech that could encourage and motivate, if only we were willing to share. The gifts of knowledge and finances, of time and talents, of caring and understanding…there are so many! Few of us possess them all, but each of us possesses at least one. Our giving helps others gain control over the circumstances of their lives.

Sharing is also God's way of helping us gain control—control over selfishness that tempts us to spend all we have on our own pleasures… control over the impulse to dismiss those with so much less as not deserving of our time, effort, and resources…control over the inclination not to get involved.

The rewards are many! Just ask anyone who, like Scott, gives generously to those in need.

What to Wear

Wear a smile and have friends;
wear a scowl and have wrinkles.

George Eliot

What you put on your face in the morning can reduce stress. No, today's reading isn't a pitch for a particular brand of face cream or make-up, but a shout-out for a smile. Hokey? Yes, but a smile works when it's worn!

Our inner stress doesn't stay inside, but goes right to the face—tightened jaw, furrowed brows, and frowning lips. We might not even realize how tense we are until we find ourselves snapping at someone's well-intentioned remark, or over-reacting to a minor glitch or inconvenience. When it seems as if everything's out of control, chances are it's our stress-level that's out of control.

What good does a smile do? A smile forces you to relax your face—to loosen your jaw, curve your lips in the other direction. While you're doing that, you might even move your neck and shoulders, and perhaps take a few deep breaths. Ahh! A smile, once on the outside, goes to the inside. A smile reminds you that, with God's help, you will get through. It's like a physical sign of a spiritual truth—it's not all up to you. God is there for you.

A relaxed face won't necessarily take away what's causing your stress, but it will make you feel capable of handling it (because you are). And when you wear a smile, you won't only feel better, but you'll discover that a simple smile is a free and easy way of looking better, too!

A God Mystery

Let mystery have its place in you;
do not be always turning up your whole soil
with the ploughshare of self-examination,
but leave a little fallow corner in your heart
ready for any seed the winds may bring.

Henri-Frédéric Amiel

If you're a mystery buff, you know the storyline. A crime is committed, and no one can solve it. Somehow your favorite detective gets involved. Through meticulous clue-chasing, your sleuth puts the pieces together, and finally the complete picture emerges and the perpetrator is caught. While you're engaged in the story, you don't mind not having all the answers. You're content to learn as the story progresses, and you're confident that everything will make sense in the end.

When it comes to spiritual things, we're up against a myriad of mysteries. Why doesn't God make everything clear to us? Why won't He answer all our questions? Why hasn't He taken away evil, eliminated hardship, and removed sickness, fear, pain, and worry from our lives? Much remains a mystery.

Just as we trust the writer of a good mystery story to lead us to the answers, we can trust the creator of our lives to reveal His answers when the time comes. Meanwhile, we can relax and savor the mystery, knowing God is in control. He sees the complete picture, and what's happening now is His way of leading us to it. Why ruin a good mystery by grasping for answers before the last chapter?

You have questions, and many will remain a mystery—a good mystery. A God mystery.

Ideal Idea

A little kingdom I possess, where thoughts and feelings dwell;
And very hard the task I find of governing it well.

Louisa May Alcott

Take a few minutes to think about the last time you lost control of a situation…or of yourself. Later, you realized that you could have done better. You could have, for example, asked for more information before jumping to a conclusion, delayed the decision, or not responded until you had regained your composure.

Now run through the scene again, but this time, imagine acting the way you wish you had acted in the first place. Picture yourself coolly evaluating the facts, even if people around you are hysterical with fear. Envision yourself calmly saying (to others, to yourself) that you need time to consider before making a choice. Hear yourself speaking softly and gently in a situation that has never failed to rile you.

God's Spirit, at work in your heart, provides the power you need to gain control over those passions that are not working for you and your relationships. In place of unruly emotions, He plants restraint and moderation. When human feelings flare, He brings the cooling waters of peace and serenity.

Rerun your in-control role until it's firmly planted in your mind. This is the ideal you! The next time you're about to lose control, let the idea of your ideal take over. At first, you might not be able to reach your complete ideal, but you're working toward it. After some more practice, the ideal you will become the real you!

Here and Now

Our grand business is, not to see what lies dimly at a distance, but to do what lies clearly at hand.

Thomas Carlyle

Business consultants and organizational experts emphasize how important it is to prioritize our daily to-do lists. They have found that employees and managers alike often spend prime working hours doing non-essential tasks instead of focusing on immediate needs. By the end of the day, deadlines are eight hours closer, but there's still no progress on the important project!

In our personal lives, we easily fall into the same habit, especially when faced with a seemingly endless list of demands, responsibilities, and urgencies. We find ourselves doing whatever grabs our attention at the moment—like browsing the Web—while important-to-the-day tasks get put off until tomorrow…or the tomorrow after that.

When you're under pressure, take a tip from the corporate world. Make a list of everything you must do—call the plumber to fix a leaky faucet, make an appointment to see your dentist, visit a friend who's in the hospital. Also include things that don't have a deadline, but are important to you—like trying a new recipe, planting spring bulbs, mopping the kitchen floor…or browsing the Web.

Prioritize each item, ranking time-sensitive tasks (must do today!) first; your important tasks but not immediate tasks, second; your like-to-dos, third. Now you're ready to start working down the list, beginning with first-ranked to-dos.

(Here's another tip: Every day, rank prayer at the very top!)

Given the Circumstances

I claim not to have controlled events,
but confess plainly that events have controlled me.
Abraham Lincoln

The American Civil War shaped the presidency of Abraham Lincoln. Though he dreaded the possible breakup of the United States and deplored the bloodshed of battle, the Civil War happened. It was his to handle, and he didn't shirk the challenge. Instead he chose what he believed to be the wisest course of action given the circumstances. It was within his power to control his response, but not the situation he was called to face.

We, too, face situations far beyond our control. The economy tumbles…natural disaster strikes...we lose a job through no fault of our own…a loved one passes away. Though we lack power to change or even alter these events, they will change us, either for the worse or for the better. For the worse? Give up. Escape. Abuse drugs or alcohol. Live in denial.

For the better? Lean on God to help you face the challenge. Spend time in prayer and meditation, asking God to strengthen your endurance. Remain faithful to your deepest beliefs and values. Seek counsel from experienced people—those who have learned how to deal with difficulties effectively. You will come through not only knowing more, but being more mature, responsible, and self-confident. Let your given circumstances control your life not just for the better, but for the best!

Meant to Be

Seek not that the things which happen should happen as you wish; but wish the things which happen to be as they are, and you will have a tranquil flow of life.

Epictetus

The morning had been a frustrating one. No milk in the fridge for her cereal. A lengthly debate with herself about what to wear. A frantic, last-minute search for the car keys. When Karen finally got to the gym, she was already running ten minutes late for her spinning class.

But if she hadn't been late and parked at the back of the lot, she wouldn't have crossed paths with another woman—a woman with sadness etched on her face. Karen came up beside her and recognized her as another gym member. As they continued across the parking lot, the woman poured out her grief to Karen, and Karen offered what words of comfort she could. After their class, Karen suggested they have a cup of coffee together. From that day on, the two women shared a warm and caring friendship.

Sometimes random delays, inconvenient to-dos, and unexpected hindrances put us exactly where God intends for us to be. Like Karen, we meet someone—a friend, a neighbor, even a stranger—who needs a listening ear and word of encouragement. Though such fortunate encounters don't occur every time we're off our usual schedule, they happen often enough to help us accept life's minor frustrations with patience and openness. Then we can look back with a smile of gratitude and say, as Karen later did, "Some things were just meant to be."

Cause and Effect

In this world, everything changes
except good deeds and bad deeds;
these follow you as the shadows follow the body.

Ruth Benedict

It's the law of cause and effect at work. Common examples—we spend beyond our budget, and then complain that we just can't make ends meet. We regularly cut short the hours of sleep we need, and then wonder why we feel so tired all the time. We neglect the worrisome squeals and knocks coming out from under the hood, and then we're surprised to find ourselves stranded on the highway a couple weeks later.

In many cases, we think we can avoid the predictable consequences of our actions. But sooner or later, negative consequences follow. And that's good, because until we run into them, we're emboldened to stay on a risky course and suffer worse consequences later. Cause and effect is an unforgiving teacher, but sometimes it's the only way we learn!

In the same way, how we treat others—with severity and selfishness, or with kindness and compassion—carries predictable consequences. Our own lack of consideration for others has the effect of making us less agreeable to others, and so they avoid us. Then we wonder why.

But your gentleness and generosity, helpfulness and caring have consequences, too—good ones. Godly ones. People remember the kindnesses you do for them. They appreciate how accepted, worthwhile, and important you've made them feel, and they're eager to return the favor. Blessings bring on blessings—it's a matter of cause and effect!

He Knows the Territory

Commit thy way unto the LORD;
trust also in him; and he shall bring it to pass.
Psalm 37:5

Doris is driving in a city she's never visited before. Though she came armed with a map, she soon realizes that she must have taken a wrong turn somewhere. No street name she sees matches one she can find on her map, and she begins recognizing landmarks she passed a few minutes ago. She's driving in circles! She decides to stop and ask directions from someone who lives there. Someone who knows the territory.

You don't have to be driving a car in an unfamiliar city to find yourself going around in circles when it comes to spiritual things. Confusing directions send you every which way, but you aren't finding what you're looking for—peace of mind. Order. Stability. Control. Just like the hapless driver, the only thing you would like to do at this point is stop and ask directions from someone who lives there. Someone who knows the territory.

God is more than someone who knows the territory—He created the territory! He has given you the gift of life, and He has mapped out for you work to do, and people to care for, to care about, to love. Whenever you're lost, He meets you with guidance and direction. Wherever you find yourself, He's there to bring you back to the place where you belong.

He's someone who knows the territory of your heart—because He lives there.

Will Power

Some who have no knowledge of the subject
say that to surrender to the will of God is an act of weakness.
They should try it and see for themselves.
They would then find that they had taken on "a man's job,"
and there is no life that calls for so much courage and faith
as that which seeks to be led according to the will of God.

Henry Thomas Hamblin

"If at first you don't succeed," the saying goes, "try, try again." We're reminded to not give up, to persevere despite setbacks, to keep on trying—good advice, except when what we're trying to accomplish is our will for ourselves, but not God's will for us.

Though it's not always easy, especially at first, to discern our will from God's will, the difference soon becomes apparent:

- Our will has its source in our dreams and imagination, but God's will most often stems from our real-life experiences and opportunities; and never contradicts what He has commanded or promised in Scripture.
- Our will is marked by our insistence on getting what we want for ourselves. Even a noble, selfless sacrifice might not match our life's purpose! God's will is made known to us when we're ready to surrender our personal desires and fully accept His desires.
- Our will leaves us anxious and fretful; try, try as we might, we never manage to grasp what we so ardently desire. God's will brings peace and fulfillment as we move forward on His path, giving control where control belongs. Joy lies in the act of following Him.

If at first you don't succeed, try again—but not your way, God's way.

The Winning Life

I began to understand that the promises of the world are for the most part vain phantoms, and that to have faith in oneself and become something of worth and value is the best and safest course.

Michelangelo

In old-time westerns, the good guys always won. Though the bad guys would get their moment of apparent victory, the fellow in the white hat saw that they got their comeuppance in the end.

In the real world, though, it seems just the opposite. Cheaters get top prizes at the expense of those who play by the rules. Fabricators are listened to, and truth-tellers are doubted. Self-indulgence is admired, but self-denial is considered dull and outdated. Do the "good guys" always win? Yes, they still do.

Dishonesty, deceit, and lack of personal self-control may provide an advantage for a time—even a long time. Yet all the while, there's the fear of being found out...the likelihood of lifestyle-related accidents, illnesses, debt...the potential shame and embarrassment of public downfall. Not a winning way—or a very tranquil way—to live!

God wants us to win where it counts, so He has given us rules to guide us and commandments to correct us. He does not want us unknowingly or carelessly sacrificing permanent victory for temporary glory. Instead, He desires to give us what the "good guys"—whether they're admired, reviled, or simply ignored—possess all along: Self-respect. Honorable reputation. Blameless conscience. Peace of mind. Those qualities always win.

No Place Like Home

There is nothing like staying at home for real comfort.

Jane Austen

No matter where you live, your home environment either supports or undermines your physical well-being. For your safety, you don't set roller skates on the stairway or stretch electrical cords across the middle of the living room. For your good health, you separate cleaning fluids from fresh foods, laundry detergents from tonight's dinner. For your security, you keep your doors latched.

The same holds true for your emotional well-being. If your surroundings distress you, you're likely to feel tense, unhappy, and out of control in your own home. But only you know the kind of environment that would relax, uplift, and inspire you! One person finds shelves of knick-knacks, pictures, and memorabilia warm reminders of favorite people and happy times. Another craves simplicity, finding peace in the visual stillness of minimal décor. Bright, dynamic colors energize some; subdued, quiet colors nurture others.

Your spiritual well-being depends on a supportive environment, too. Regular quiet time to read and reflect on God's Word creates a place for your soul's rest and refreshment. The habit of prayer increases your reliance on God for your daily needs, and the ability to listen to His voice surrounds you with His wisdom and strength.

What would make your environment more supportive of the warmth, rest, and peace of mind you need? Whatever you choose—lively and dynamic, quiet and tranquil—let God and His love reside in the center of your home and your heart.

Inner Peace

Do not lose your inward peace for anything whatsoever, even if your whole world seems upset.

Francis de Sales

It's possible to spend years, even decades, searching for inner peace. Some people pick up and move to an idyllic spot in the world where they imagine they can enjoy a carefree, trouble-free existence. Others pour over sacred texts from the East and from the West, hoping to pick up the one golden nugget of truth that will open to them the secret of personal serenity.

Many more have given up. With all the chaos around us, they say, how can anyone realistically hope to achieve inner peace? Yet inner peace is possible. It's not found or accomplished by our action, however, but given to us by God's action. His peace never depends on our circumstances, but comes to us despite our circumstances. It doesn't dissolve, but deepens, when times get rough and we cry out for peace of heart and mind.

Inner peace is a gift of God, one God desires for you. Your trust in Him and reliance on His wisdom lifts the burden of fear and worry from your heart. As you lean on His strength, you come to realize that no hardship in the world even approaches His power to see you through. Instead, He walks with you, lifting you above the ordeal you're experiencing now. In His arms, there is your deep and lasting peace.

Mind and Body TLC

I find, by experience, that the mind and the body
are more than married,
for they are most intimately united;
and when one suffers, the other sympathizes.

Lord Chesterfield

Most of us realize that when we get sick, we need to treat ourselves with a hearty measure of TLC. We may take a day or two off work, ask someone to watch the kids, postpone appointments, or simply take it easy until we're feeling better.

Few of us, however, give the same kind of care to a burdened, fatigued, worry-sick mind. No, we stubbornly keep to our daily routine, even though mentally feverish with anxiety. We bravely soldier on, despite nagging cares, chaotic emotions, and sleepless nights. Is it any wonder, then, that physical illness follows? It's as if the mind is screaming, "If you won't listen to me, perhaps you'll listen to what your body's telling you!"

When we ignore lingering pain, we decrease our chances of diagnosing and treating a disorder in its early stages. Similarly, when we ignore prolonged mental tension, we lay ourselves wide open for confused thinking, diminished ability to make rational choices, and susceptibility to a number of physical ailments.

If your mind is filled with anxiety, you have a symptom. Bring your feelings, thoughts, and emotions to God. Let Him show you how to get your symptom under control. Let the Great Physician treat you with His healing TLC.

Undefeated by Circumstances

When we see ourselves in a situation
which must be endured and gone through,
it is best to make up our minds to meet it with firmness,
and accommodate everything to it
in the best way practical.

Thomas Jefferson

"It's business as usual for me," Anita informed her staff. But no one who heard her announce her recent medical diagnosis believed it would be "business as usual" going forward. Treatments, tests, and visits to an out-of-town clinic would surely keep Anita from her usual long hours and selfless dedication to the people around her.

Everyone, however, admired Anita's spunk. She was determined not to let the hurdles ahead defeat her before she had even met them. "I have an amazing physician," Anita went on to say, "and she outlined everything I can expect in the coming months. It looks like a lot—it is a lot," she admitted, "but all I ask is for God to help me make it through each day, one day at a time."

Every morning, Anita prayed for strength to handle today's test...today's fatigue...today's doctor's visit. Although she was distressed to find that it wasn't "business as usual" for her, she was overwhelmed to find how willingly her staff members put in extra hours and took on additional work so she could be away without worry.

Six months later, Anita, fully recovered, stood up in front of her staff. "Never before have I realized how kind, supportive, and encouraging people could be," Anita said with tears in her eyes. "My diagnosis was a blessing—and so is each one of you."

Up Close and Personal

*Of all the things which wisdom provides
to make life entirely happy,
much the greatest is the possession of friendship.*

Epicurus

All of us know people we call acquaintances. Though we may see them fairly regularly, we wouldn't claim a deep friendship with them. A lasting bond never develops for a number of reasons—difference in outlook, age, experience, interests. Yet our acquaintances are part of our lives, and we enjoy chatting with them when we happen to meet them.

Unfortunately, many of us treat God as an acquaintance. Though He longs for an up-close-and-personal relationship with us, we keep Him at arm's length. Sure, we like knowing Him and feel good about having Him around, especially when things aren't working out very well for us. A lasting bond never develops, however, because we fail to let it happen. Why? Perhaps we're not sure if He really cares about us...we're not willing to spend much time with Him...we're not really interested in making Him the center of our lives.

You know where this is going! Yes, God yearns for more than staying one of your acquaintances. He has opened Himself to friendship—a deep, lasting, life-changing, up-close-and-personal friendship. Despite the strength of His desire for your friendship, however, He leaves the level of your relationship with Him in your hands. You have complete control—He loves you that much.

Of Time's Past

Regret is an appalling waste of energy;
you can't build on it; it is good only for wallowing.
Katherine Mansfield

You've heard people say it: The past is the past. Yet letting go of the past isn't always easy. We clasp close to our hearts memories of happy times with loved ones now gone, often shutting ourselves off from the possibility of happiness yet to come. We allow the shadow of past mistakes to follow us far into the future, hindering ourselves from finding joy and satisfaction in who we are and where we are today.

Letting go of the past is far from denying it. Of course you fondly remember the people you have loved, as well as the years and circumstances you found fulfilling—those times when you felt most vital, alive, and productive. Your life has been blessed, and you can celebrate it! But why let those memories keep God from blessing your life today, and tomorrow, and the day after? You have room for more memories of laughter, joy, and love!

At the same time, you regret your failings, some of which may have resulted in lifelong consequences. There's nothing you can do to change what happened; but you can allow the memory of having failed in the past to increase your reliance on God, who is quick to forgive. It's in your power (because He gives it) to use yesterday's mistakes as a springboard to a stronger, wiser you.

The past is the past. The best is yet to come!

What a Difference!

Courage is the greatest of all the virtues,
because if you haven't courage,
you may not have an opportunity to use any of the others.

Samuel Johnson

When we're feeling depressed and unhappy, it takes courage simply to get up in the morning! After all, why would you want to, when all you're expecting is more of the same—chronic fatigue…ongoing problems…onerous responsibilities…tedious tasks? And more often than not, you will get what you expect.

More courageous than getting out of bed—and far more satisfying—is the courage to expect better. Expect more from the day. Before you lift your head from the pillow, give yourself less "same old, same old" and more "what a difference a day can make!" Imagine yourself alert and attentive instead of tired. See yourself discovering solutions to problems, happily managing your responsibilities…doing what needs to be done with a smile. Have greater expectations, and watch yourself get what you expect.

There are challenges in your life, and it takes courage to face them down each day. And no, they aren't about to go away anytime soon. With God, however, you have the strength it takes to stand up under their burden and the pluck it takes to go through the most difficult trials. But no matter what the day is bringing you, refuse to accept "same old, same old." Ask Him to show you what a difference a day can make!

Plain Brown Bag

God is able to bless you abundantly.

2 Corinthians 9:8 NIV

Ever noticed that the tonier the store, the fancier the bag? Along with soft music, elegant environment, smiling sales associates, designer clothes, and lofty prices, you get a chic handle bag to hold all your purchases. Don't you feel a little lift to your step as you walk down the sidewalk, your classy bag at your side?

Apparently God didn't get the memo on recommended bag designs. He surrounds us with awe-inspiring beauty—blue skies, starry nights, snowflakes and dewdrops—but we don't even notice. He showers on us (for free!) priceless blessings—love, joy, contentment, friendship—yet we think they're nothing special. He graciously serves us with compassion and gentleness, and He hands it all to us in the "plain brown bag" of an ordinary day!

There's no surprise, really, to find God working with and among ordinary things—and ordinary people. He wants you surrounded by His presence, so He comes to you daily, wherever you are. He wants you to recognize Him as the giver of all our blessings, so He richly blesses you every single day. Do you feel a little lift to your step...boost to your confidence...warmth to your heart as you go through your day, your compassionate God at your side?

If you need reassurance that He is there with you, don't look for Him in the fancy stuff, but in the ordinary. His richest blessings arrive most often in an everyday, common, plain brown paper bag.

The Eyes Have It

Could we change our attitude, we should not only see life differently,
but life itself would come to be different.
Life would undergo a change of appearance
because we ourselves had undergone a change in attitude.

Katherine Mansfield

What do you see? Right now, it's possible that you're viewing nothing but problems ahead. Challenges seem to come right after another, and despite your best and most resolute efforts, you can't seem to get things under control. So what do you see for tomorrow? Nothing but more struggle, disappointment, and discouragement!

But there's another way of looking at your todays and your tomorrows, and that's with the eyes of faith. Faith allows you to see your life more as God sees it—purposeful, essential, and full of hope. Your life, including its struggles, shortcomings, and limitations, was known by God from before you were born. He saw your disappointments before you did, and He was there to comfort you. He knew you would be discouraged at times, and He has always been there to lift you up. And He knew you would come to today, wondering why you feel so helpless.

Perhaps God permits these things because He knows He can use them to build your strength, your endurance, your self-confidence—and most importantly, your faith in Him. What if…instead of a struggle, you see a challenge you can meet with God's help… instead of disappointment, you see another door God has opened for you… instead of discouragement, you see an invitation to come to Him…what if? Today would look very different. And so would tomorrow. Do you see it?

The Roller Coaster

Sorrow is a fruit. God does not allow it to grow on a branch that is too weak to bear it.

Victor Hugo

Doug's tests, procedures, and hospital stays have gone on for nearly a year as he tries everything possible to fight a rare blood disorder. Some weeks, the treatments take effect, and he feels well enough to drive again, go to church, and join his pals for coffee. Perhaps he's won the fight! But then on other weeks, complications arise. He's back in the hospital for another round of tests. Recovery retreats to a distant possibility. "It's a roller coaster," his wife says of this difficult time.

What good news lifts up, bad news sends crashing down…again and again. Anyone who has gone through the experience knows. Hopeful signs vanish in an instant, only to flower again after another attempt, another go at making a miracle happen. It's a roller coaster. "If it weren't for our faith," Doug and his wife tell their friends, "there'd be no way we could get through this."

Because both Doug and his wife are leaning on God's strength, they're able to receive the good news with glad thanksgiving and the bad news with humble acceptance. The ordeal has brought them closer in a way they never thought possible. They have learned to cherish the days they have together, celebrate family times with special appreciation, and find, through it all, the care and compassion of a loving God.

Faith empowers you to ride all the roller coasters life sends. There's no peak, dip, or curve you (and God) can't handle together.

Always Open

I will never leave thee, nor forsake thee.

Hebrews 13:5

OPEN. It's a welcome sign in the window of our favorite shop or café. "I'm open to your ideas" is an encouraging and flattering phrase to hear. "My door is always open" are inviting words from a dear friend we'd like to visit.

Of all God's many characteristics, His openness is something we often overlook. When we run into trouble with finances or relationships, we tend to believe that there's nothing God can do about it. When worry weighs heavily on us, we're fooled into thinking that God's ears are closed to our concerns. When we're sick, fearful, or depressed, we imagine His healing love is unavailable to us. Closed.

But God is open—always open. It's the way He is! He willingly opens His arms to receive you when difficulties come your way, no matter where they have come from or who's at fault. He lifts you up to Him so you can get a better perspective, and He helps you meet life's challenges. He gladly opens His ears when you share your anxieties with Him, and He listens when you pray. He graciously opens His heart to you—a heart that receives you whenever you call on His love.

Open! It's a welcome sign of His goodness…an encouraging word to hear…an invitation from your God to you.

One Step at a Time

Great things are not done by impulse,
but by a series of small things brought together.
Vincent van Gogh

Jill woke with a start. "What am I going to do about getting everything in the house packed?" she panicked. The clock on her bedside table flashed 2:00 AM. Already her hectic schedule allowed for scant free time, and now her head throbbed at the prospect of moving. Yet if she wanted to keep her job (and she did), she was required to transfer to another city. For hours, she tossed fitfully as her mind churned with all it would take to manage this major and unexpected upheaval in her life.

The next day, an exhausted Jill confided to a co-worker. "But Jill," the co-worker said, "nothing's happening until this time next year, and maybe later. Thank goodness they announced it now and we've got time to get organized!"

In many cases, we, too, know ahead of time. And when we do, we can start taking control of what we need to do and when it needs to get done. For example, Jill spent the early morning hours fretting about the huge job of packing everything, although she had 12 months to plan what she would keep and what she would sell or give away. Similarly, we often panic at the prospect of a major undertaking which, if stretched out over time, can be accomplished with effort and organization on our part.

When God gives you the gift of time, use it in the way He intends for you to use it. Take one step at a time. Accomplish even a small slice of it each day, week, or month. In the end, you'll be ready!

Doing One Thing Well

There is time enough for everything in the course of the day
if you do but one thing at once;
but there is not time enough in the year
if you will do two things at a time.

Lord Chesterfield

Perhaps you remember a few years back when multi-tasking was the order of the day. We were urged to take on several jobs at once if we wanted to increase our productivity and get things done. While some boasted of their ability to multi-task, others among us had our doubts. We tried it, yes, and found we did nothing very well, or very happily. We had to admit it: multi-tasking left us a nervous wreck!

Though opinions about the benefits of multi-tasking have shifted, we're often tempted to take on several things at once. Driving and talking on the cell phone is a prime example! Yes, we need to get where we're going and we need to get in touch with a friend about lunch and call the school about tonight's parents' meeting...and.... Feel the tension mounting?

A wry commentator once noted that God took it one day at a time when He created the world. Even He didn't do everything at once! What's more, He declared a day of rest after He completed His work. There's a message in God's example for all multi-taskers out there—and for anyone who prefers to do things well...and happily, too.

Released from Fear

The Lord is my light and my salvation;
whom shall I fear?
Psalm 27:1

When life gets out of control, we feel as if we're groping around in the dark. We reach out blindly, hoping to grab something we can hold onto, but nothing's solid. Nothing makes sense anymore. Soon, because we don't know where we're headed, we're scared to take another step in any direction. Fear has us firmly in its grip.

If you have ever felt paralyzed by fear, you know it's not easy to escape it. You don't know whether or not a certain action will get you out of the situation, or lead you further in. While others confidently offer advice, nothing they say feels quite right for you. Here in this dark place, you're not only alone, but on your own.

In truth, though, you're not alone and you're not on your own. In the middle of this darkness—in the place you most fear—is where God meets you with the comfort of His presence. He releases you from the bonds of fear by saying to you, "Here's my hand. Take it." And with that gracious invitation, He leads you away from the darkness of anxiety, worry, and distress. With Him showing the way, you can once again walk with certainty and confidence.

Each step you take with Him brings you closer and closer to where He wants you to be—in His light.

Getting It to Work

Results? Why, man, I have gotten a lot of results.
I know several thousand things that won't work.

Thomas Alva Edison

Though Thomas Edison is most famously known as the inventor of the electric light bulb, he held over a thousand U.S. patents for devices as disparate as a motion picture camera and mechanical vote recorder. Over a century ago, he even developed a battery for a working electric car!

He managed to invent what worked, however, only by inventing countless things that didn't work. He never would have found success with even one design had he not been willing to turn around when he hit a dead end and try another path. Another dead end? There was always another path…another approach…another detail to add, change, or eliminate for a different, and perhaps successful, result.

When you're at your wit's end thinking of ways to get things under control, take a tip from Edison. You might try one thing only to find it really doesn't work for you. But that's not to mean something else won't work out beautifully. Second, third, or fourth crack at it, and still no satisfaction? As Edison might say, "Why stop there?"

Imagine yourself at a workbench putting different pieces together, taking them apart, and putting them together another way. That's the way it is when you're working to get things under control in your life. So now you know what doesn't work. What will work for you could come together with your very next try. (Let God give you a few hints!)

You as Decision-Maker

You are the one who must choose your place.
James Lane Allen

Others make decisions for us all the time—if we let them. No, it doesn't take a particular person standing in front of us, telling us what to do and how to do it. If that were so, our solution would lie in standing up for ourselves and telling our would-be puppeteer to cut the strings!

Instead, we have hidden decision-makers. They're concealed in messages that lead us to believe we must look a certain way if we want beauty...act a certain way if we want popularity...own certain possessions if we want status...do certain things if we want a fulfilling life. But if we blindly follow these decisions, we exert no control over where we're going.

Decision-making messages hide inside us, too. They emerge in feelings of shame or unworthiness or pessimism, and then these feelings determine our reality—if we let them. That's why God lives inside our hearts as a defense against thoughts, feelings, and emotions that would drag us away from Him. It's His decision to free us from decisions and decision-makers that work against us, frustrate us, and propel us in all the wrong directions.

Whether the messages are coming from the outside or the inside, let God cut the strings. Let Him free you to take control of your decisions...of your life...of you.

Forgiveness in Control

He is a very green hand at life
who cannot forgive any mortal thing.

Robert Louis Stevenson

Do you ever forget how much you are loved? Your spouse misses a milestone anniversary…your best friend doesn't notice your latest achievement…your kids are oblivious to how hard you're working so they can live comfortably.

At times like these, it's easy to imagine that no one cares, and we can do nothing about it. Yet neither claim is true. People do care, but sometimes they fail to show it. An onerous workload, burdensome problems, and youthful self-centeredness are only a few of the reasons others may fail to meet our expectations. And there's something we can do about it. While resentment pushes them away, making it harder for them to show their love for us, forgiveness draws them closer. Forgiveness softens our feelings, puts the matter into perspective, and lovingly reminds them that we need to hear the words "I love you"…"I admire your work"…"I'm grateful for all you do."

God forgives, and His forgiveness draws you closer to Him where you can say the words He longs to hear: Words of delight in possessing a growing, living, vibrant relationship with Him…words of wonder for all His creation and the ways He works in your life…words of gratitude for all the blessings He pours out on you every day.

Forgiveness puts love in control of your heart.

Seeing Is Believing

A thousand words will not leave so deep an impression as one deed.

Henrik Ibsen

There's no controlling a rumor. Our protestations to the contrary only amplify the rumor's claim. As soon as we set the record straight with one person, two others show up with the story on their lips. And despite what we say, unfortunately some will give more weight to the rumor.

What words cannot do, however, actions often can. The woman shunned as a result of gossip has little chance of successfully refuting the story. But she can choose to hold her head high as she goes about her day, letting her good actions silence another's hateful comments. The man ignored because of hearsay may not be able to disprove what's being said about him, but he can conduct himself with openness and honesty until others realize the tale was false.

If you have ever been the subject of a rumor, you no doubt remember how powerless you were to control it. Yet no matter how true or untrue the things said about you, God can see the ache in your heart. Where there is fault, He is ready to forgive; where there is pain, He is ready to comfort; where there are wounds, He is ready to heal.

Even faced with injustice, you have the strength of knowing yourself as a beloved child of God. Act with confidence, because seeing is believing.

A Question of Confidence

I am not afraid of storms,
for I am learning how to sail my ship.
Louisa May Alcott

The person who's most confident, goes the quip, simply doesn't know what's going on! We smile, but most of us nod in agreement, too. We're confident until we find out everything that could go wrong (and probably will). A few frustrations, and confidence goes out like a candle's flame in a windstorm.

The shining light of our confidence fades quickly when we imagine we can take on the world all by ourselves. Then reality sneaks in. Ask the new mother home alone for the first time with a fussy infant. Ask the conscientious office worker suddenly promoted to manager of a large department. Ask the shy, quiet volunteer invited to stand up in front of everyone and say a few words. Ask any one of us face-to-face with something we know, deep down inside, we just can't handle. So much for taking on the world!

When your confidence depends not on your own capability, but on God's ability, you have confidence that stays alight. Confidence in His presence gives you someone to call on when reality overcomes your power to cope. Confidence in His strength provides you with support when you need it, and encouragement to continue on, to grow, to take on your world. Just don't try it without first placing your confidence firmly in Him!

The Perfect Response

*A person without a sense of humor
is like a wagon without springs–
jolted by every pebble in the road.*

Henry Ward Beecher

Have you ever helped a stressed-out bride-to-be plan her wedding? If so, you might know the term "bridezilla"—that is, a young woman who decides that everything must be perfect on her special day. Not leaving anything to chance, she drives everyone else to distraction as she checks, rechecks, tweaks, and changes everything from the color of her flowers to the shade of her lipstick.

Despite months of fussing and fuming, bridezillas rarely get their "perfect" day. Rain sends the garden ceremony indoors. The flower girl comes down with the measles. The musicians arrive ten minutes late. All the stuff of frenzy now, but admit it—rich fodder for laughter later!

Few of us plan out days with a bridezilla's obsessive attention to detail, but we often expect perfection. No underdone turkey at Thanksgiving. No rain during a summer picnic. No unforeseen expense, unwanted advice, or uncomfortable moment after we've said something we shouldn't have. (Oops!) But let it ruin a "perfect" day? Fly into a frenzy trying vainly to "fix" it? No, there are other responses—perfect responses for imperfect days. Responses that come from a heart of acceptance, peace, and God-infused joy.

Unlike bridezilla, you know that what's really important is not the daily gaffs and glitches, but a lifetime of love and laughter. (The more glitches today, the more laughter ahead!)

God's Daily Blessings

When I first open my eyes upon the morning meadows and look out upon the beautiful world, I thank God I am alive.

Ralph Waldo Emerson

A thick slice of scrumptious chocolate cake. An ice cream sundae topped with a tower of fluffy whipped cream. Chunky fudge brownies that melt in your mouth. Add your own super-indulgent dessert to the list!

God's blessings to you are even richer, more delectable, and more extravagant than the most mouth-watering concoction you can imagine. And unlike the occasional sweet treat, you can take a big serving every day without feeling guilty! So do you?

Sometimes we ration God's blessings more strictly than we ration candy bars. Instead of opening the morning with thanksgiving for the beginning of a new day, we let fear or anxiety hold us back from delight. Rather than going about our day expecting the best and believing He will help us handle the worst, we walk around with very, very serious looks on our faces. We miss the sunshine, the birdsong, the sound of the wind through the trees. We restrain ourselves from simply enjoying an afternoon. We restrict the number of people we greet, the moments of fun we take, the breaks from routine we allow ourselves. On this kind of diet, it's no wonder we're feeling a little grumpy!

God's blessings are yours for the taking. If He didn't think you deserved them, He wouldn't put them right in front of you. The best news of all: There's not a single calorie involved! Just pleasure—pure pleasure. Enjoy!

He Watches Over

The Lord is my shepherd...
He leadeth me beside the still waters.

Psalm 23:1, 2

Have you ever watched a small child in a corn maze? He tries to navigate through rows and rows of corn that tower a foot or more over his head. Some paths take him through and out again, while others lead him deeper into the maze, and still others are dead ends.

Sometimes, after trying several paths that go nowhere, the child, scared, begins to cry. That's when a watcher, perched high above the corn rows, sees him and calls to him. He sends one of his helpers into the maze to comfort the child and show him the way out and into the comforting arms of his mother.

In a way, we're like the small child, scared and lost. We begin walking in one direction, only to discover that we're not closer to where we want to go, but further away. We change paths, but this one isn't right either—we hit a dead end, and now we need to start over. Of course we're frightened! Of course we wish someone would show us the path that leads to our goal!

God, like the maze watcher, sees. When He hears us call out to Him, He sends help. Perhaps a friend to listen and give us perspective so we can see which direction to go. Perhaps someone to counsel and encourage us, providing us with the motivation to try another route. Perhaps a word from Scripture to guide us along the right path.

At a loss to know which way to turn? Look up. God knows exactly where you are.

Spiritual Lifesaver

The majority of men live without being thoroughly conscious that they are spiritual beings.

Søren Kierkegaard

If you have ever gone on vacation and forgotten to ask someone to water your houseplants, you came home to some pretty droopy specimens! Leaves, brown around the edges, have turned from glossy to dull. Where vibrant blooms once filled the air with fragrance are withered and crumbling petals. Right away you water the dry, cracked soil and add a little plant food. Day after day you watch them, prune them, and keep them well-moistened. Soon, leaves perk up and regain their healthy sheen. Old blooms are gone and new flowers begin to bud. What once appeared completely unsalvageable has been saved because you cared. You took the time to bring them back to life.

When we abandon prayer, Scripture reading, and meditation, we get spiritually droopy. Left to our own thinking and reasoning, we become increasingly dull to God's presence and His work in our lives. Our "blossoms" of love, joy, and peace wither away, and in their place self-centeredness, discontent, and anxiety take root. Our spiritual life looks iffy at best.

But here's the difference between ourselves and those neglected houseplants—we're never unsalvageable! No matter how long a soul has gone without God's nurturing touch, His nourishing food, and His compassionate care, God's love sees life. He will cultivate even the driest ground and enrich the poorest soil so seeds of faith can take root and souls flower with beauty, health, and vitality.

No matter how long it's been, God will take the time to make your spiritual life bloom again.

Inspired by a Dream

Keep away from people who try to belittle your ambitions.
Small people always do that, but the really great
make you feel that you, too, can become great.

Mark Twain

A little girl, taken to the ballet for the first time, sits enthralled as the music swells, the curtains part, and a wonderland of castles, cottages, tulle, and tiaras opens in front of her. Her eyes widen in amazement as the prima ballerina seemingly floats onto the stage. The dancer leaps, glides, and pirouettes with flawless precision and grace. "Wow!" the girl whispers to her mother. "I wish I could do that!"

To her, the ballerina on stage is someone from another world—a world of beauty, wonder, and elegance. She can only imagine herself among the flitting, fairy-like dancers. Certainly with years of dedication and practice, she could be there; but right now, it's only a dream.

Do you look up to someone? A religious leader whose message inspires thousands…a physician whose work brings health care to impoverished people…a philanthropist whose donations improve lives the world over. Have you ever wished you could do the same thing?

The girl's youth and inexperience prevent her from realizing her dream, just as circumstances beyond your control may hinder you from doing exactly what the person you most admire is doing. Yet, inspired by a dream, you can follow. Maybe you won't reach millions of hurting people, but you can reach one, two, or three. Maybe you aren't in a position to donate billions to a worthy cause, but you can give five, ten, or twenty dollars.

God uses people to inspire other people. Who inspires you?

Jitter Reduction

When we are unable to find tranquility within ourselves,
it is useless to seek it elsewhere.

François de La Rochefoucauld

Tranquility and commotion don't go together. Say we're dealing with upheaval in our lives or the lives of loved ones…rushing constantly from one place to the next…or simply have too much to do in a day…whatever it is, turmoil outside of us quickly turns to unrest inside. In a way, we're like sponges, soaking up all jitters coming our way!

For inner calmness and peace of mind, there are some jitter-reducing things you can do:

- Eliminate or limit activities that keep you on the run for too many hours of the day.
- Decide which problems are yours to solve, as opposed to problems others must solve for themselves.
- Avoid situations that compromise or offend your beliefs and values.
- Respond to the world as it is with lightheartedness, humor, and acceptance.

No matter what you do, however, upsetting and disturbing events will still happen. No one can control everything! That's why the most important jitter-reducer is this one:

- Spend time with God. Put your trust in God's presence, His compassion, His care, His wisdom every day.

Allow yourself to soak up the peace He has to offer. Breathe deeply! The more room you make for Him inside your heart, the less room there is for worry and anxiety. Rest calmly in Him. And it's more than likely that the world around you will start looking a lot less jittery, too!

A Trip down Memory Lane

Ask, and it shall be given you; seek, and ye shall find; knock, and it shall be opened unto you.
Matthew 7:7

Spend a few moments thinking back to a time when you hoped for something, and then got what you wanted. Perhaps things like earning a good grade in a difficult class in school...applying for and winning a sought-after position in the workplace...saving the money that enabled you to remodel your home or go on a great vacation...solving a difficult problem...overcoming a significant challenge. How about when the one you had your eye on asked you out...the child you longed for entered your family...the friend you can always count on is there for you—again.

Memories of times you have wanted and obtained, planted and reaped, hoped for and gathered in serve to remind you that God has blessed you richly. He has given you the commitment it takes to work toward goals and achieve them. He has opened doors of opportunity for you, and you have walked through them. He has heard your prayers, and He has said "Yes" to you more often than you can count.

Whenever you're tempted to think that you can't, or that it's useless to try, let your good memories tell you otherwise. Let the proof you have of God's favor in the past remind you that you have His favor now, because God's love for you never changes. He has blessed you yesterday, and He will today and tomorrow, too.

Standing on the Edge

To leap across an abyss,
one is better served by faith than doubt.
William James

Ever have one of those days? You feel so frazzled that it would take just one minor mishap to send you right over the edge!

Go ahead and jump—right into God's arms. He has the strength to catch you and the power to lift you up from the depths of discouragement. In His hands, you feel His calming touch and hear His soothing voice telling you—assuring you—that yes, He knows. Yes, He has it all under control. Reliance on God's presence, His strength, and His compassion is your bridge from utter hopelessness to solid confidence... from complete confusion to faith-filled patience...from jangled nerves to lasting peace of mind.

Sounds easy, doesn't it? But of course it isn't. We're used to thinking that we have to handle everything. That we should be able to face down whatever life throws at us. But what about when we try and try, but fail? Then we start feeling down on ourselves. Really easy! What's hard is turning our day and everything in it over to God. It takes faith, God-given faith, that He will help you through whatever the day may bring.

The next time you think you're going over the edge, put yourself—no, throw yourself!—in God's strong arms. You will find them more than capable of lifting you up!

Prayer Is the Answer

Pray in the Spirit on all occasions
with all kinds of prayers and requests.
With this in mind, be alert and always keep on praying
for all the Lord's people.
Ephesians 6:18 NIV

Prayer—it's so easy that a child can do it, yet so shrouded in mystery that the oldest and wisest among us cannot understand how it works. We wonder what difference prayer makes. Do our prayers persuade God to change His mind in any given circumstance? Does whether or not we pray affect the outcome of events around us? Does it matter how we pray—alone or with others, in time-honored words or spontaneous phrases?

God may not choose to answer all your questions about prayer, but He is inviting you to pray. Whenever you lift your thoughts to Him in faith, you are communicating with your heavenly Father, who hears the words of your lips and the yearnings of your heart. He is open to whatever you want to tell Him, whether it's to thank Him for a blessing or beg Him for His comfort in tough and troubled times.

When you pray for physical and material blessings for yourself and others, God welcomes your wishes and tenderly regards what you say. He answers according to what He knows is best. When you pray for spiritual things like a stronger faith and increased trust in His wisdom, He promises to say "Yes." Whatever your prayer is about—from global events to personal problems, from life-altering situations to little changes that would make life easier for you—God listens. If it matters to you, it matters to Him.

The Most Important Thing

The conclusion is always the same: love is the most powerful and still the most unknown energy of the world.

Teilhard de Chardin

There's an adage any real estate agent will tell you: The three most important things to consider when looking for a new home is location, location, location. In a similar way, it might be said that the three most important things to consider when looking for your spiritual home is love, love, love.

You'll know it when you see it, because genuine love from a God-filled heart is a lively, active love. Though we might feel impatient or aggravated, love answers kindly and gently. When we're tempted to insist on our own way, love opens us to compromise and cooperation. Despite our inclination to turn things to our own advantage, love reminds us of the needs of others. Love teaches us how we can help make a difference for the better in their lives.

This love doesn't stand idle when it comes to spiritual things, either. It compels us to actively and energetically nurture our relationship with God by meeting with Him in prayer and listening to Him in the words of Scripture. It compels us to put Him first in our thinking, follow the path He has laid out for us, and accept His will in our lives.

It matters where your heart resides. When you make love your spiritual home, you've staked your claim to prime real estate.

Good Intentions Gone Astray

To understand everything is to forgive everything.

Proverb

Most of us have had bouts of foot-in-mouth disease—and for some of us, on more than a few occasions! What we thought was a witty quip was taken as an offensive comment. What we offered as a friendly greeting was received as an annoying remark. Our motives were good, but the outcome? Not so good. We never have control over what others hear, and they can't read what's in our hearts.

Perhaps you can recall a time when you acted with the best of intentions, thinking you were saying what needed to be said, or that you were doing someone a great favor, but the whole thing misfired. Or you might have gone in one direction, believing it to be God's will for you, and only later finding out otherwise. Because God knows the yearnings of your heart and the reasoning behind your words and actions, He understands your motives. You never need worry He will misconstrue the meaning of what you say to Him. Even if what you do turns out to be the wrong thing, He will not reject the good intentions that led to your choice.

And remember always: Just as God forgives us when we have the best of intentions but stumble badly, we are compelled to forgive others when their well-meant comment stings or kindly proffered witticism hits us the wrong way. Foot-in-mouth disease affects us all. Forgiveness is the cure.

God's Great Light

Give light and the darkness will disappear of itself.

Erasmus

Was it a UFO? Or were those lights we saw sweeping across the night sky a passing plane, clever hoax, or natural phenomenon? There's no telling sometimes!

In the shadowy darkness of our limited understanding and spiritual innocence, we can find ourselves gazing at false lights—people who claim to possess a higher wisdom, but have only high-flown assertions. False lights, including human-devised theories about God, can sweep into our lives. Through emotional appeal and the promise of great things ahead, we give over control of our spiritual lives to them. Only too late do we realize that their light is only a dim reflection of the real thing—the light of God's Word.

Rather than seizing control of you with ingenious gimmicks, God lovingly persuades you to follow His light by revealing who He is, how He has worked in and among people just like you, and what He asks of you as His cherished son…His beloved daughter. In His light, you will grow in understanding of God's ways. Gradually, your spiritual shadows disappear, replaced by the warmth and comfort of His presence.

You may not know for sure about those strange lights you saw in the night sky—but you can know for sure who's shining God's light. Those are the people who point not to themselves, but to God and His Word, the Bible.

Never Too Far Away

God loves each of us
as if there were only one of us.
Augustine

Augustine, who was born in an upper-class family in present-day Algeria, lived in the latter half of the fourth century. Though his mother raised him as a Christian, the teen-aged Augustine abandoned the faith and pursued a pleasure-seeking lifestyle with worldly friends.

In his 30's, Augustine, teacher and scholar, was inspired to reread the Bible. Immediately he was struck by passages about how God's message of love and forgiveness has the power to transform people—even someone like him! He was baptized. Today, he is widely known for donating his sizable inheritance to the poor, and for his life as a forceful and influential defender of the Christian faith.

God may not have such a dramatic outward transformation in mind for us, but He definitely desires to make an inward change. Through the working of His Spirit in our hearts, He yearns to grant us control over negative thoughts, willful impulses, and volatile emotions that keep us away from Him and off the path He has planned for us. Strengthened and inspired by God, we can leave the burdens weighing us down and go forward with peace of mind and heart today and for all our tomorrows.

No matter where you are, God reaches out to you with His soul-deep transforming power. Augustine was not too far away, and neither are you.

Why Me?

Why are you troubled because things do not succeed according to your desire?
Who is there who has all things according to his will?
Neither I, nor you, nor anyone on earth.

Thomas à Kempis

We get to our car after a tiring day and discover a flat tire...we're just finishing an important project and the computer goes bonkers... we rush to the airport and find that the flight has been cancelled. "Why me?" And with those words, perhaps a mental scowl toward God, who, after all, controls all things, doesn't He?

Of course He does. Nonetheless, He permits us to experience the common irritations and annoyances that are part of life. He also allows us to experience love and laughter, delight and satisfaction, ability and achievement...happy times with family and friends, heart-warming memories, and hopes for the future...the aroma of freshly baked cookies, and the tang of sweet, ripe fruit. The companionship of a beloved pooch. The purr of a contented kitten. And not just once in a while, like those irksome flat tires, computer glitches, and airline snafus, but every day.

Why you? Because He knows you can handle the occasional hitches and hiccups—and even laugh about it later. What's really important—the love, the laughter, and all of that—He showers in abundance. Why you? Because He loves you, that's why.

Little Corners of Order

Much may be done in those little shreds and patches of time which every day produces, and which most men throw away.

Charles Caleb Colton

Laurie putters around the house. She takes a notion to rearrange the books on her bookshelf, so she does—and then sits down with a cup of tea to reread a story she hasn't read in years. Another afternoon she neatens her linen closet, and one evening she goes through her dresser drawers and pares out little-worn garments for donation to a thrift shop. She admits it: she likes to putter. She might spend an hour or more doing things not for anyone else to notice, but simply for her own satisfaction.

Does it sound as if Laurie has too much time on her hands? Actually, she doesn't. She's a super-busy woman whose calendar is crammed with responsibilities, activities, and appointments. It probably looks a lot like yours! Yet she has discovered the importance of puttering… of dillydallying…of taking time out to do small, quiet things that occupy the hands but rest the mind. Things nowhere to be found on your to-do list, but things that put a little order in your corner of the world. Things that don't always take very long to do, yet feel so satisfying to have done.

Probably a few putter-friendly tasks await you right now. A little something that will never get number one priority on your list of things to do, but something that you frequently notice and think, "Someday, I'll take the time to do that." Can that "someday" be today?

First Impressions, Lasting Impressions

What you think about yourself is much more important than what others think of you.

Marcus Annaeus Seneca

All too often, first impressions become lasting impressions. Whenever we're introduced to someone new, we're instantly struck by the person's appearance—pretty or plain…handsome or homely…short or tall… carefully dressed or casual. We take in behavior—friendly or aloof… chatty or quiet…energetic or laid-back. Then we form an opinion based on what we've seen and heard. He or she is capable, creative, witty, intelligent…or none of those things. Our desire to get to know the person better most frequently rides on a positive or negative first impression.

Sadly, negative first impressions can close us off to potentially positive and fulfilling relationships. It's true with others, and it's true with ourselves. If our childhood was marked by feelings of incompetence, we're apt to carry those feelings far into adulthood. No matter what we accomplish, we never feel we've done enough. If as a teen we believed we weren't attractive, we never take a second look at ourselves with clearer, more mature, eyes. If we were once shy, we rarely give ourselves a chance to be anything else but shy.

If you are carrying with you a negative first impression, give yourself another chance to impress, because you are impressive. God created you in His image! Smile at the awkward child, forgive the struggling teen, understand the grown-up who stumbles once in a while. Look beyond first impressions, whatever they have been. Marvel at the miracle of who you are right now—someone God loves with a deep and lasting love.

Created and Shaped

We are the clay, and thou our potter;
and we all are the work of thy hand.
Isaiah 64:8

A beloved biblical image draws a picture of God as a sculptor, and each one of us as molded and shaped in His loving hands. Unlike the clay pots a sculptor produces, however, we're not left to sit on a shelf, unchanging and motionless. Instead He has given us the power to move and do, shape and create.

Think of today as a lump of clay. What are you, the sculptor, going to do with it? You have the God-given ability to create something meaningful…something significant…something beautiful. If all that sounds out of reach, consider this: What could be more meaningful than some quiet moments with God in prayer, or a phone call to a friend who's going through a bad time? What could be more significant than a kindly smile, an encouraging word, a helping hand? What could be more beautiful than a life shaped by God-given love, peace, and joy?

God, the sculptor, has created us as ordinary people, yet each one of us remains unique in His eyes. He has put in our hands a lifetime of ordinary days, yet each one filled with unique potential, promise, and opportunity. We are the sculptors now!

The Master Sculptor invites you to manage and mold the hours by perceiving the day He has given you with the eyes of an artist. Shape the day with a positive attitude and good-for-you choices. Perhaps it's just an ordinary one, but see it as God does—another chance to mold something unique, precious, and lovely to look at!

On Hold for Now

Patience means waiting without anxiety.

Francis de Sales

"Thanks for calling. Can you hold for a minute?" With a sinking feeling, we say, "Sure." We know how often "a minute" turns into five, ten, fifteen minutes until someone picks up the line and helps us. We don't like being put on hold, and we don't like putting certain parts of our lives on hold, either.

Yet the college student who wants to succeed puts entering the workforce on hold until after he has earned his degree. The young married couple puts having a family on hold until they're financially able. The employee puts extensive travel on hold until she retires. At one time or another, each one of us has decided to put something on hold until the proper time comes. But do we enjoy waiting? Not usually.

Impatience with being put on hold makes us hang up, and impatience with having something on hold makes us act prematurely. That's when we end up with problems we could have avoided, if only we had waited until later. For example, we lose control of our bills when we jump into financial obligations before we have the income to cover them...of our time when we commit ourselves to too many activities...of our direction when we haven't prepared ourselves to meet the challenges ahead of us.

Unlike the next company you contact, God always takes your call. He loves to listen as you talk about the things you would like to do and the places you would like to go. But sometimes He asks you to put something on hold for a while. That's because He has other plans for you right now.

By Word-of-Mouth

He is truly very learned who does the will of God, and forsakes his own will.

Thomas à Kempis

Word-of-mouth has power. When considering a purchase, for example, we go for the brand a family member has bought and raves about. We're more likely to read books and listen to music recommended by people we know, and to join organizations our friends say would interest us.

There are times, too, when we have in mind something we want to do, and we check it out with friends and family. Perhaps they're cool to the idea, or warn us against it outright. Though we're clinging to our idea, we keep looking for someone to approve it—someone to slap us on the back and tell us he'll be with us every step of the way. Wouldn't it be nice if God were that "someone"?

We pray for God's approval, and because our desire is so great, we think we hear Him say "yes" to everything we're planning on doing. So we forge ahead, heedless of the fact that God never said "yes." Only too late do we admit that it was our plan all along, not His will. Our reasoning in control, not His wisdom.

Words from God's mouth come from Scripture. He may also send His counsel as advice from mature, experienced friends and relatives. His "yes" or "no" may even speak in our deepest thoughts, if only we can put aside our own plans long enough to listen.

Resolutions from the Heart

*When you have chosen your part, abide by it,
and do not weakly try to reconcile yourself with the world.*
Ralph Waldo Emerson

New Year's resolutions, it's said, are made to be broken. And how quickly we break them! By mid-January, our earnestly uttered resolutions to save money, lose weight, eat healthier, and exercise more have gone by the wayside. One reason might lie in the fact that so many New Year's resolutions we make are shoulds, wishes, or like-to-haves. They're not deep-down, genuine, 100 percent wants.

Regardless of the date, now is a good time to consider real and meaningful resolutions—not the kind made to be broken or the ones you announce to your friends at the turn of the year, but the resolves resting deep inside your heart and mind. These are changes you genuinely desire so you can become more of the person you want to be. They're promises you make to yourself so you can find more fulfillment in your life. Are they big changes or small changes? Either way, they're important changes. They're positive, practical, and doable things you resolve to do not because you have to, but because you want to.

God never gives up on His pledge to care about you and make His presence, protection, and wisdom available to you. It's not something He has to do—after all, He's God, and He doesn't have to do anything! For Him, loving you is His deep-down, genuine, 100 percent want, and it always has been and always will be.

First Love

We are bound to Him, and not He to us,
because before He was loved, He loved us.

Catherine of Siena

Here's a sure way to experience inner turmoil: try to gain God's love. Yet people attempt it all the time.

Some think they deserve God's love simply by being the smart, attractive, and talented person they are. But when something happens and they find that they're not so smart after all...that their physical beauty has faded...that their talents have failed to bring them fulfillment—then what? They doubt God's love. Yet not one of us deserves God's love through any quality of our own (a quality He gave us in the first place).

Others believe they need to earn God's love, so they embark on a life of harsh humility, sacrificial giving, and selfless acts. But there's no joy, no thanksgiving, no ability to receive for themselves God's good gifts. All the while, there's the nagging feeling of never being able to do enough, and they're right. Not one of us could ever do enough to earn God's love.

Now let's look at a sure way to experience inner peace: accept God's love. Open your arms to it. It's there for you. Because of His love, you are lovable just as you are, and the good things you do for others in response to His love are pleasing to Him. For joy...for rest...for peace, live in His love.

Time to Downsize

How much there is in the world I do not want.

Socrates

If you want to downsize your living space, you probably won't find it an easy task. There are things you've owned for decades—but do you need them now? There are souvenirs and mementoes of happy times—but will you have a place to put them in your smaller home? Perhaps there are gifts or knick-knacks that you liked when you received them—but can you really keep them forever? It's hard!

Harder yet is to discard attitudes, perceptions, and beliefs that we've kept for so long in our thoughts. Suppose, at a young age, we experienced difficult times. More difficult, perhaps, than any child should have to suffer. At the time, fear and suspicion seemed the only protection. Or suppose in later life we were badly treated by a trusted friend or a spouse. A shell of mistrust would keep us safe, so we hid behind one. Now we're so used to suspicion… mistrust…what else?...that we are hard pressed to get rid of it. Even though it doesn't fit our new lifestyle. Even though our old feelings are keeping us from embracing a fresher, healthier, and more realistic perspective.

God offers you a new stage in life—one of lightness of heart, freedom from fear, and confidence in the capabilities He has given to you. Are you ready to move in? If so, there's downsizing ahead of you. Fear doesn't fit in with the days ahead of you. You won't have room to store suspicion and uncertainty. There's no need for distress. Why would you want to keep these things?

It's not always easy to toss what you don't need anymore, but there comes a time when you want to make room for the new.

Living at Peace

Whenever you're in conflict with someone,
there is one factor that can make the difference
between damaging your relationship and deepening it.
That factor is attitude.

William James

Read most any advice column, and you will quickly discover who creates the most stress in our lives. No, it's not the acquaintance making an unpleasant comment or the stranger letting the door slam in our faces. Aggravating at the time, yes; but those who can really get our goat are the people who are closest to us—parents, spouse, adult children, in-laws, close friends, neighbors, co-workers.

Living at peace with those who are closest to us in a family, workplace, or community relationship are the most significant people in our lives. We have a bond with them, whether we see them every day or only infrequently. You can guess what it's like if that bond is weighted with past grievances and current animosity.

You can also guess how much better it would be if one person decided to lay aside yesterday's offenses and refused to carry the conflict any further. Peace would have a chance to take hold, and peace is contagious. Once peace takes hold of one person—you?—it takes hold of another person. Perhaps the irritating in-law will realize no one's responding to her behavior. Maybe the annoying co-worker will figure out that there's no one to squabble with anymore. They have only two choices available: fight with themselves or opt for peace.

But be careful—so much peace will break out in your relationships that advice columnists will be asking you how you did it!

Inspired or Tired?

Our chief want in life is somebody who shall make us do what we can.

Ralph Waldo Emerson

In many middle schools, students are asked to pick a notable person and write about him or her. Tell what the person did and why it's important. Along with gaining research and writing skills, the students discover people who have made a difference in the world or in their communities. Assignments like this encourage students to focus on what others have done and what's possible for them.

As grown-ups, we often become jaded. We've experienced more than a few of life's bumps and blows, and we know that the road to what's possible is chock full of potholes and detours, steep climbs and sharp turns. So how did this contemporary of ours achieve so much, and we so little? Notable people no longer inspire us, they tire us!

The point of admiring the achievements of others, however, is the same for us as it is for middle schoolers. God has a special path for each one of us, and it isn't necessarily parallel to the one He has laid out for someone else. In His eyes, faithfulness counts more than fame, and embracing His will—whatever it is—is the only way that leads to fulfillment and peace.

Who inspires you? Give thanks for that person, and let his or her achievements encourage you as you discover all that's possible as you walk God's special path for you.

Must Have It—Or Not

Before we set our hearts too much upon anything, let us examine how happy those are who already possess it.

François de La Rochefoucauld

Ever get that just-gotta-have-it feeling? Few of us can avoid a bout of gotta-have-it occasionally, surrounded as we are by glossy ads in magazines, vivid graphics on TV, and bright billboards lining our highways. What's more, it's so easy to get what we gotta have—a click away on the computer, or block or two down the road at the nearest big-box retailer.

But when our desire to possess bigger and better things gets out of control, we find ourselves focused more on what we don't have and less on what we do have. Just-gotta-have-it takes over! Soon, we're all but blinded to the blessings we enjoy every day and the great spiritual riches God has in store for us. We're grasping to get things rather than opening our arms to receive what's right in front of us.

God has placed us in a society where material things are prominent, plentiful, and appealingly advertised. We thank Him for the many comforts and enjoyments readily available to us! Yet with abundance comes the temptation to let possessions control our thinking, our values, and our peace of mind. We ask Him to help us moderate our desires…to not always need the biggest and best…to learn contentment and gratitude for what we have.

Sometimes just-gotta-have-it isn't as good as just-gotta-leave-it.

Minor Accumulations

Sunshine is delicious, rain is refreshing,
wind braces us up, snow is exhilarating;
there is really no such thing as bad weather,
only different kinds of good weather.

John Ruskin

Minor exasperations can drive us to distraction. At the end of a day of constant interruptions, silly glitches, and petty annoyances, we're utterly worn out. "So what all happened today?" we're asked when we get home. Yet anything we mention sounds trivial, because on its own, it is. And then to hear, "I just don't understand why you're so upset" is only the latest of those niggling nuisances!

We allow insignificant exasperations to accumulate almost without thinking, but what would happen if we treated little pleasures the same way? If we gathered together the gift of a new day, the aroma of hot coffee, the company of friends over lunch, the laughter of a child, the familiarity of home, the comfort of a good dinner, the enjoyment of a favorite movie—would all of this drive us to gratitude? If to the question, "What all happened today?" we mentioned the tasty sandwich we had for lunch instead of the phone that rang ten times in the space of an hour—would that make a difference?

What we let accumulate in heart and mind each day matters. The morning's events we choose to remember and mention affect the way we feel in the evening, and possibly all night long. What we say about today can turn it from draining to energizing, exasperating to funny. Best of all, it changes us from fault finders into joy creators!

Miracle-Working Prayer

Prayer does not change God,
but changes him who prays.
Søren Kierkegaard

You've heard it said that prayer works miracles. Do you think it's true? Because not everyone thinks so.

Consider the distraught mother who prays that her rebellious son will come to his senses. He doesn't. Or the skilled worker who prays for a job opening, but interview after interview, he's turned down. Or the severely injured young woman who prays for healing, yet never fully recovers her health. We can identify with their feelings of defeat and disappointment, and we can understand it if they conclude that God has let them down. Has he?

"Yes, He has let them down." That's the answer we'll hear from those who would use prayer as a tool of control. Though they may not even realize it, they pray for the outcome they want and then sit back, expecting God to snap to it and perform according to their wishes. When He doesn't, there's a problem—but whose problem?

"No, He has not let them down." These words come from the lips of those who understand that prayer is not a means for us to control God, but to open us to His control. As we lay out our burdens to Him, He works in us to strengthen us and encourage us. When He doesn't choose to act the way we would like Him to, He gives us the ability to gratefully accept His better and wiser choice for us.

That's the miracle of prayer!

Right-Side Up

In the light of eternity, we shall see that what we desired would have been fatal to us, and that what we would have avoided was essential to our well-being.

François Fénelon

It may have been a long time since you've had occasion to stand on your head, but no doubt you remember what the world looked like with your feet in the air and your hands on the ground—completely upside down!

In a way, upside down is how we see the world when we look at it from a human perspective. We long for a comfortable, problem-free life…hope for instant and easy success…pray for good health, fulfilling relationships, and financial security…yearn for control over what people expect of us and say about us. While it's natural for us to value all these things, God has other values and standards. He sees the world and our lives from His perspective—right-side up.

As much as we wish difficulties wouldn't come our way, we have to admit that without them, we'd have no reason to reach out for God's help and His strength. We'd never really get to know Him if everything we wanted came at the flick of a finger, and we'd never really be able to share in the sufferings of others if we never once suffered an illness, a setback, or a hardship ourselves. If we possessed complete control over the events of our lives, our limited vision and insight would very likely lead us to disastrous consequences.

With your feet firmly planted on the ground and your heart securely rooted in God's love, you can start seeing right-side-up!

Random Acts

The best portion of a good man's life is his little, nameless, unremembered acts of kindness and love.

William Wordsworth

You've heard about random acts of kindness. Say you're in a fast-food drive-thru lane, and you pay for the order of the person in the car behind you. No strings attached. Just a little act of blessing given to a stranger who has no way of paying you back, because you're three blocks away before he even knows what you did.

Have you ever done a random act of kindness for the person closest to you—yourself? This is different from a reward, like the chocolate nugget you promise yourself after you've cleaned house, finished the laundry, or mowed the lawn. It's different, too, from a short nap you might allow yourself before a long evening, or a luxurious bubble bath you treat yourself to after hard pysical work. A true random act of kindness has to be, well, random. With no strings attached.

Examples? How about these for starters:

- Compliment yourself on a job well done.
- Give yourself a break from the day's duties.
- Take time out to think, sing, read, draw, pray.
- Bless yourself, your home, and your loved ones.

In a way, God's blessings to you are like random acts of kindnesses. He showers them on you every day not because of something you've done for Him, but just because He wants to. No strings attached!

A New Beginning

In all change, well looked into,
the germinal good out-veils the apparent ill.
Francis Thompson

Lisa's fifty-fifth birthday marked a new beginning for her. Newly single and with her two children out of the house and on their own, she decided to move into a smaller home, enroll in a few adult education classes, and get a complete make-over at a local day spa. After she had done what she had set out to do, she felt (and looked) like a new woman!

Though Lisa initiated, planned, and remained in charge of her new beginning, not all of us find ourselves in such a favorable position. Say we're blindsided by a life-altering event, a loved one's unexpected change of plans, or a shift in circumstances we could never have foreseen. Nothing we initiated or planned, for sure, but what about being in charge?

No matter what has happened that we can't control, here's what we can control—how we choose to use it. Like a person standing at the start of a bridge, we can gaze longingly back at what used to be… or we can go forward, cross the bridge, and allow a new beginning to unfold in front of us.

Difficult new beginnings—unexpected and unlooked for—are neither easy nor fun. We may need to grieve what has gone before we're ready to embrace what's ahead. Rest assured that God understands and cares. Walk with Him across the bridge and let Him bring you to your new beginning today.

The De-Cluttered Day

Simplicity, simplicity, simplicity!
I say let your affairs be as two or three,
and not a hundred or a thousand.

Henry David Thoreau

When homeowners sign on with a real estate agent, one of the first things the agent might advise them to do is remove clutter from tables, shelves, and cabinets. That's so when potential buyers walk through the house, they're not sidetracked by those cute baby photos (awww!) or distracted by the vase they knocked to the floor (oops). The agent wants them focused on things that matter—room size, special characteristics, and general appearance.

In a way, we're like those potential home buyers as we go through our day. What do we notice first—trivial details or substantial features? Are we wasting our energy on avoidable glitches and frustrations—like that shattered vase—or have we prepared for the day by making realistic plans and setting achievable goals? In short, are we spending our time and attention on things that count, like our genuine concerns...our spiritual growth...our relationship with others and with God?

De-cluttering isn't only for hopeful home sellers. Our lives become cluttered with too many obligations and commitments, interests and pursuits. Perhaps we have handled a huge number of activities in the past, but we're not managing as happily now. We've changed. As with household items we no longer use or enjoy, it's time to hand them on, to let them go, and to focus on what counts now.

De-cluttering is for all of us who tend to gather, gather, gather instead of simplify, simplify, simplify.

The Gifts Within

Let us remember that within us
there is a palace of immense magnificence.

Teresa of Avila

If you were to name gifts people have given to you, you'd probably look around you and point to the cashmere sweater from your favorite cousin...hand-sewn apron from your little granddaughter...sparkly earrings from your best friend. You can't help but smile as you recall all the given-with-love tokens and mementos you've received over the years!

But what about gifts not merely around you, but in you? All the gifts God has showered on you, beginning with your first breath? And then there are all the other gifts you possess, thanks to Him...gifts like abilities and talents...interests and achievements...hopes and dreams... good memories and life experience. He has given you the gifts of growth and maturity, of increasing joy, faith, and security in Him. Without your even asking, He provides the comfort of His presence no further away than your own heart.

If it has been a long time since you've taken a look at all the inner gifts you have, why not spend some time thinking about them now? Don't be modest when you consider your kindness, gentleness, and service to others. Never downplay the gifts of joy and laughter, and don't forget the ability to comfort and the capacity to feel and experience love.

You can't help but smile, can you, at the gift that is you? Thank You, God, for everything!

Got a Minute?

Time is a very precious gift of God;
so precious that it's only given to us moment by moment.
Amelia Barr

At some point in life, most of us learn not to waste money. Perhaps our parents taught us to save our allowance and spend it only on worthwhile things. Or maybe, as we got out on our own, we made a few foolish purchases which we later regretted. From then on, we've been less impulsive spenders. Perhaps rising prices and living expenses made us revamp our spending habits, and now we're much more careful with our financial resources.

Usually it's later in life that we learn not to waste time. Far from imagining we have all the time in the world as we did when we were younger, now we realize we don't. No one does. We start focusing more on things worthwhile to us and less on things others say are important, or on things that were important or necessary in the past. We're increasingly confident saying "no" to commitments we really don't want to make, and unapologetically comfortable spending our time, whenever possible, in exactly the way we choose.

How do you feel about the time God has placed in your care today? Do you know how valuable it is? It can't be accumulated, stored, or put away for later. It's more valuable than gold or any other resource the world has to offer. And God has given it to you right now.

Needs and Wants

Nothing troubles you for which you do not yearn.

Cicero

Needs and wants—there's a big difference, isn't there? We need food, and we want gourmet cheese and imported cookies. We need clothing, and we want the latest styles and designer labels. We need a break from work, and we want a European vacation. Though our needs may be few, our wants are limitless!

If we take an objective look, we'll find that God has supplied our needs. We have food to eat and clothes to wear. When we need a break from work, we have a home to relax in, a neighborhood to explore, and nearby places to visit. Is there lack? He strengthens and guides us, protects and defends us. He provides what is most needed. We have all we need for a contented and happy life.

It's the wants that give us fits. Our wants keep us striving to get more rather than discovering the luxury of living with less. They agitate and aggravate as we struggle to fulfill our desires and make our wishes come true. But what if our wants aren't what God wants for us? What if He says, "You have everything you need for right now"?

Peace of mind and a contented heart go together. They make themselves at home in those who can separate legitimate needs and limitless wants—those who can trust God to generously provide the one and lovingly decide about the other.

From Madness to Peace

Trouble and perplexity drive me to prayer,
and prayer drives away perplexity and trouble.
Philipp Melanchthon

Where is your day most likely to go haywire?

For some, the madness begins first thing in the morning with the rush to get the kids up, fix breakfast, take a shower, find a missing shoe, and grab the car keys. For others, it's bumper-to-bumper traffic…the spate of phone calls and emails every day…trying to put dinner on the table for a testy family when we're tired and hungry ourselves.

Our daily routine isn't always flexible, and there are some things that aren't changing anytime soon. The kids need to be at school at a certain time. We need to answer calls and reply to emails. We want to provide dinner for the family most nights, if not every night. But preparation can ease the stress and help us gain some measure of control over the haywire parts of our day. Things as simple as laying clothes out the night before… getting food ready ahead of time whenever possible…using public transportation instead of driving…prioritize phone and email messages… eating more frequently to avoid hunger-induced headaches and quick tempers at the end of a long day…and remembering that humor helps in any situation.

Perhaps one of these practical steps will help you prepare for the day ahead. Here's another spiritual step, and it's the most practical of all—pray. Put your haywire moments into God's hands. Thank Him for each one, because they mean He has provided you with privileges and responsibilities. With Him, you can turn madness into peace.

Doing What We Love

The highest reward for a man's toil
is not what he gets for it,
but what he becomes by it.
John Ruskin

Work is essential to our wellbeing. In home, office, store, factory, or plant, our day-to-day obligations, at the very least, give us a good reason to get up in the morning! Paid or unpaid, our work compels us to communicate with others, use our talents and skills, and give of ourselves to the people we meet and the tasks at hand.

Many among us are privileged to be doing work we love. There's nothing else we'd rather be doing, be it managing a home or running a conglomerate. Yet despite the benefits and rewards of having work to do, not all of us can claim that we love doing what we're doing. Not all of us are able, financially or otherwise, to give up what we're doing now and pursue an occupation we believe we'd like better.

How do you feel about the work you're doing? If you love it, give thanks to God for giving you the gift of being able to live your dream every day. If you feel less than loving toward your daily work, keep in mind what your work is making possible for you—a home, comforts, the ability to care for your family and those who depend on you. And then focus on your work itself. You may not love all of it, but can you love some or part of it? From there it's only a small step to loving more of it.

Loving What We Do

Most folks are about as happy as they make up their minds to be.

Abraham Lincoln

"I came here kicking and screaming," Melanie admitted. Though her husband was eager to move to a warmer climate, Melanie wanted to stay in the home they had shared for the past 30 years. Their children had been raised there, and each room held cherished memories for Melanie that no place else ever could. Her husband won out, however, and the couple settled in a Florida golf community. "And now I love it!" she laughed.

Sometimes the "bad" things life hands us—whether through a loved one's wishes, a job-related requirement, unplanned-for family responsibilities, or other turn of events—are blessings in disguise. Maybe it means leaving a place or position when we'd honestly prefer to stay…changing our lifestyle to accept responsibility for a grandchild, parent, or elder relative…spending time, money, and energy to help someone with physical, emotional, or mental needs. These are the things we take on "kicking and screaming," because we'd really rather not deal with them—but we do.

Perhaps you know someone who's been there, or you've been there yourself. You prayed that God would ask someone else. He didn't. You did it, because you were convinced it was the right thing to do. You began to discover some good things. You warmed to the whole idea. Eventually, you may even have come to love it!

Anything Goes?

Gratitude bestows reverence,
allowing us to encounter everyday epiphanies,
those transcendent moments of awe
that change forever how we experience
life and the world.

John Milton

Many thoughtful commentators have noted a marked lack of reverence in our culture. We're on first-name terms with teachers, doctors, and ministers… public and in-home behavior is practically indistinguishable…Sunday-only suits and dresses are almost nonexistent. Anything goes!

While carried to an extreme, formality causes distance between people, lessening our ability to identify with others and their viewpoints. Lack of any formality, however, robs us of the ability to feel and show the uplifting quality of reverence.

No, we can't (and wouldn't want to) turn back the clock. But each of us can do a little bit to reclaim reverence for ourselves and for those around us. We can dust off a few of the lessons we learned in kindergarten, like saying please and thank you…treating others with civility and kindness…dressing in a way that shows we respect who we are, where we are, the people we're with…living with a sense of gratitude for all the blessings God gives us every day.

It's like this: How can we expect to revere God in heaven if we can't revere anyone or anything on Earth? How can we admire Him, but admire nothing or no one He has made? Reverence isn't required anymore, but it can be learned and practiced by anyone who wishes to experience its rewards.

The Topmost View

Change is the watchword of progression.
When we tire of well-worn ways, we seek for new.
This restless craving in the souls of men spurs them to climb,
and to seek the mountain view.

Ella Wheeler Wilcox

"When things start going downhill," someone has said, "don't go right along with them!" But sometimes it's hard not to join the southward slide. One disappointment shadows how we view the next opportunity, and our misgivings set the stage for yet another disappointment. A single change in our lives upsets us, and in response, we let go of the comfortable and comforting habits and routines that haven't changed at all. It's time for us to put the brakes on the downhill ride!

How you respond when things start getting away from you makes the difference between a futile chase to capture what's gone and a fertile period of prayer, reflection, and repositioning. Even the most heartwrenching turn of events contains the seeds of new life. Change and disappointment in one area of your life leaves an opening for other chances and opportunities. But you won't find them if you're running after the past...regretting what cannot be undone... bemoaning what lies beyond your control.

If you're tired of the downward slope you find yourself on, take hold of the hand God graciously stretches out to you. He has the strength to lift you back up to the top of the hill, where you see more clearly, discover your blessings, and reclaim the direction of your life.

A Spiritual Home

Thou art my rock and my fortress.
Psalm 31:3

Katie reached midlife and still didn't know what she wanted to do. After she left school, she tried various career paths…teacher, marketer, medical assistant, health counselor, dance instructor. She took on each role with enthusiasm, but after a short time, her passion ebbed and she started looking around for something else…something else, she thought, that would better suit her talents and interests.

As you can imagine, her spiritual life followed the same course. Seeking a belief system that would connect her to God, she eagerly took whatever path presented itself to her, only later to discover that she felt no closer to God than she did while she was skipping along on the last path.

Katie is fictional, but her dilemma is real. It's the story of any one of us who has not found our life's purpose and our spiritual home from an early age. As if we're in a clothing store where no sizes are marked, no styles and colors separated out, and everything lies jumbled on a table, we're frantically picking up each shirt, pants, and dress, hoping against hope to find something that we like.

In the Bible, God reveals Himself as a rock…an anchor…a fortress. As our rock, He remains immovable; and as our anchor, He holds us steady. As our fortress, He keeps us safe and protected from the storms of a turbulent and ever-changing spiritual life.

If you're searching and have not found Him, stand still. Rest in Him, because He has found you.

A Powerful Truth

Power will intoxicate the best hearts…
No man is wise enough, nor good enough,
to be trusted with unlimited power.

Charles Caleb Colton

In real life and in TV dramas, there's the character with the big ego who amasses a huge fortune and now gleefully wields control over the lives of family members, friends, and employees alike. Of course, everyone suffers. Most certainly in fiction, and most often in reality, the fiendish tycoon's downfall comes. Control-obsessed people usually find that they're not so powerful after all.

While vast control is the stuff of movies and a few individuals, we're not immune to wishing we could exert more control over our lives and the lives of those around us. Without malicious intent, of course! No, if we had control, we'd control for the better. We'd open doors that have been closed to us for so long. We'd provide help and relief to our family and friends (and get the stubborn ones to do what we think is best for them). But we're beginning to look like the egotistical tycoon, aren't we? It's simply a matter of scale!

Our trust in God's wisdom pulls us back from the natural desire to control, even for the better. He's the only one who knows what's better, despite our best efforts or reliance on human reasoning. He promises to give us everything we need to handle whatever happens, when it happens. Now there's our real control!

The Worry Connection

Take therefore no thought for the morrow: for the morrow shall take thought for the things of itself.

Matthew 6:34

"Let tomorrow take care of itself!" Sure. We hear a friend tell us not to worry, we resent the admonishment—how could she know what we're going through? We tell ourselves not to worry, and we dismiss our own rebuke. We seem to be wired for worry!

But "let tomorrow take care of itself" are words from the lips of Jesus as He speaks to us about those things He has put into our hands, and those things He asks us to leave in His hands—like tomorrow. He gives us today's work and responsibilities to take care of…today's challenges to overcome…today's problems to solve, all with His guidance and direction.

Most importantly, God daily offers us all the spiritual nourishment we need. While we fret about what we'll eat tomorrow, God invites us today to love, trust, and believe in His willingness and ability to provide for us. This is what He has for us right now! Will we miss all this—something to enjoy right now—and instead agonize about tomorrow? And not one of us has any idea what tomorrow will bring!

If feel like you're wired for worry, ask God to break the connection. With Him first in your heart and mind, you'll have nothing to worry about. Absolutely nothing!

A Good-to-You Day

Be willing to have it so.
Acceptance of what has happened
is the first step to overcoming
the consequences of any misfortune.

William James

Sometimes you have a bad day. Nothing seems to go right, and on top of everything else, you're hit with terrible news. A friend confides to you that she and her husband are considering divorce, and you hurt for both of them…the headlines blare the details of a shocking event, and you feel sick at heart…you find out that your income will be drastically reduced by the end of the year, and you have no idea how you're going to accommodate the shortfall.

Bad days come to everyone from time to time. When they come to you, take control of your response by turning bad days into good-to-you days. Set aside special alone time with God so you can express your deepest feelings. Pray for those who are most affected by the news that burdens you. Read and meditate on Scripture, listening for the words that speak to you with caring, compassion, and direction.

A good-to-you day includes putting off, as much as possible, decisions and tasks you'd normally take care of. If you can, pull away from routine and do something that gives you time to think through what you've heard, to manage your emotions, to focus on what happened, to get more information before reacting to events.

Bad days happen. A good-to-you day is one you create.

Rest Assured

As soon as you trust yourself,
you will know how to live.

Johann Wolfgang von Goethe

We wear a mask, hoping no one will know how insecure we really feel. We don't measure up to other people…to where we are…to how we've always imagined ourselves at this age. After all, we're not high schoolers anymore! But the self-assurance that eluded us when we were teens trying to discover ourselves still escapes us. Sure, we have a little more polish and know-how than we did then, but still we feel the same. We don't measure up.

Can you relate to a few of those thoughts? They're thoughts common to many, regardless of age, experience, or accomplishments. If you have ever heard someone you admire for her achievements confess to you her feelings of inadequacy, you know. You wondered why and how she could possibly feel that way with so much evidence of success. With so much to be proud of. With so much to live for, love, and enjoy.

Your response might, in some small way, give you an idea of how God looks at you when your sense of self-assurance runs low to nonexistent. "Why?" He asks. "When I created you for a purpose and gave you the ability and talent to accomplish everything I have in mind for you!" Yet He has compassion on your fears, and He expresses His care for you by promising His presence, His help, and His strength in all you do.

You don't need the mask anymore, because you're assurance comes from inside—and whatever shines inside is guaranteed to glow on the outside!

A Modest Proposal

You have a good many little gifts and virtues,
but there is no need of parading them,
for conceit spoils the finest genius.
There is not much danger that real talent or goodness
will be overlooked long,
and the great charm of all power is modesty.

Louisa May Alcott

The word "modesty" evokes pictures of women in high-necked blouses and long skirts. Because of the old-fashioned image it conjures up, modesty has been largely discredited. Yet when we think about what the word really means, we're left to wonder whether modesty isn't a quality we desire. If modest, perhaps, isn't something we'd like said of ourselves.

Modesty and humility go together. Like humility, modesty doesn't shout about itself or try to get attention by showiness or boastfulness. It doesn't spend time thinking of ways to win applause, impress people, or make itself known by whatever means possible. Modesty has reserve, like humility; both would wait for their accomplishments to be noticed rather than point out their work to others. And if no one notices? That doesn't matter. Their efforts, their service, and their love is the same.

This is a far cry from high-necked blouses and long skirts, isn't it? For sure! Genuine modesty has too much self-respect for outward displays of modesty. Instead, it's marked by quiet decency, steady honesty, selfless generosity, and God-given self-control.

Does modesty sound appealing to you? Think about it—and no maxi skirt required (unless you like to wear one, of course)!

The Forgiving Friend

We set up harsh and unkind rules against ourselves.
No one is born without faults.

Horace

"Nobody's perfect!" we often say when we fumble in front of others. Behind the easygoing remark, however, we're cringing. We're not taking the matter lightly. Instead, we're scolding ourselves for being such a klutz…such a dummy…and surely that's what everyone else is thinking, too, we add!

No doubt you've heard a dear friend say something she shouldn't have, or you were there when she messed up big-time. You saw her face redden with embarrassment, listened as she tried to sweep away her words, watched as she tried to put right what went wrong. Did you decide she was a klutz or conclude she was a dummy? Certainly not. Instead, you felt for her, and did what you could to ease her through an awkward, uncomfortable moment.

What you would do for a friend, why not do for yourself? Treat yourself with the kindness you treat others. It's what God does for you when you stumble. He doesn't accuse you or call you names. Rather, He sympathizes with your discomfort and extends His hand of forgiveness. He lifts you up, dusts you off, and assures you of His continued love and care.

You can depend on God's tender understanding and kindly support when you stumble. He has shown you how He treats you so you can treat others the same way—including yourself.

A World on View

What we see depends mainly on what we look for.
John Lubbock

What do you think God looks for? Imagine Him scanning the Earth and all the people in it. Where do you imagine His eyes linger? Because God reveals Himself as a loving God, it's easy to say His eyes would linger in places where love is present. Because He's compassionate, He would favor scenes of compassion. The same with kindness and tenderness, forgiveness and understanding. He looks for these things, He finds them, and He delights in them.

Similarly, we're drawn to people, acts, and events that reflect our qualities and perspective. If we're confused, angry, or anxious, we look around us and find only more confusion, anger, and anxiety. Then we're convinced that we're right to feel the way we do. It's as if the whole world is a mirror of our attitude!

And the opposite is true. When God-given love, trust, and peace fill the heart, we find ourselves surrounded daily by people and acts of love…by reasons to trust in the goodness of life…by opportunities to discover and experience soul-deep peace. What we see builds up more love, trust, and peace within us. Again, it's as if the whole world is a mirror of what's in the heart.

What do you look for? Invite God to fill your heart with His goodness, kindness, and love. Then go through your day and take note of what draws your attention. You might be in for some very pleasant memories!

All the Proof Needed

Now faith is the substance of things hoped for, the evidence of things not seen.
Hebrews 11:1

Somewhere along your spiritual walk—if not in many places along the way—you've probably asked God for proof.

Proof, say, of His existence, or of His powers, or of His care for you as an individual person. How about a physical appearance to put the matter at rest? Suppose, for instance, a miraculous intervention in your life or in the lives of your loved ones? "God, could You do that?" we ask. "If you do, then I'd believe without a doubt in the world—and so would everyone else!"

God answers by giving us something better than the proof we ask for. Instead, He provides us with life and breath. He gives us the capacity to experience joy and laughter, love for others and hope for the future. He enables us to discover strength in struggle, peace in turmoil, goodness where wickedness appears to prevail.

What's more, He walked the Earth in the person of Jesus, who lived and spoke His truth. He performed miracles of physical and spiritual healing and feeding. He lifted the burden of guilt from heavy hearts, bringing peace and order back to their lives. But still, some asked for more proof. "Do this, do that," they shouted, "and then we'll believe!"

When you ask for proof, let Him give you something better—faith.

A Balanced Life

To go beyond is as bad as to fall short.
Proverb

No one wants to be the wallflower at the dance and longingly watch everyone else have fun. But what happens when we're so afraid of being the wallflower that we're compelled, like the belle of the ball, to kick up our heels without stopping? What happens when we feel we can never sit down?

We're in an action-oriented society. We admire those who go out and get things done, and we're praised by others when we initiate action and carry it through. We like people who are out there, not those sitting on the sidelines! Yet both places have their pitfalls. If we stand idly by while others take on the challenges of making a difference in their lives and in the world, we're missing the pleasure of using our talents and the thrill of reaching meaningful goals. If we feel bound to accomplish too many objectives, however, we're quickly overwhelmed by a dizzying number of responsibilities.

Balance in both the spiritual and physical life comes with moderation. Enough goings-on to keep us joyful, alert, and connected with others… enough quiet time for prayer, renewal, and reflection. Enough giving to learn selflessness, generosity, and compassion…enough receiving to learn humility, appreciation, and gratitude. Enough reaching out into the world for maturity, experience, and sharing…enough reaching into the soul for wisdom, strength, and understanding.

Are you a wallflower or the belle of the ball? For a balanced life, try both.

Thanksgiving and Praise

I will praise the name of God with a song,
and will magnify him with thanksgiving.
Psalm 69:30

When we received gifts as children, our focus was on the gift. Sure, we knew to say "thank you" to the gift giver, but as soon as the words were out of our mouths, the gift received our full attention.

Only as we got older did the gift giver become more important than the gift itself. A small trinket someone gives us for a birthday reminds us how much her friendship means to us. Something as simple as a necklace or pair of earrings, while lovely, could never match the beauty the giver has brought to our lives. It's not the gift (although aren't gifts great?) but the giver that's most important.

God, the giver of all the gifts we enjoy, hears our thanks. Yes, He listens as we tell Him how much we appreciate all that we have and name those special things we're especially happy to have received. But only as we mature in our spiritual lives do we realize there's something more important than the gifts—the Giver.

Even more awesome than the gifts He gives is the reality of His being who He is—God! God who created the universe, who rules over it, and who yet has the desire to love and care for each one of us!

"Thank You, God" is a prayer of appreciation for all He has given to you...and "I praise You, God" is a song of gratitude for all He is.

Good Foundation

Seek ye first the kingdom of God,
and his righteousness;
and all these things shall be added unto you.
Matthew 6:33

"It's going to fall," her grandmother warned. Yet the child continued to put one block on top of the other until—it fell. All the blocks lay scattered around her as her grandmother's words echoed in her ears.

Without even realizing it, we often take on one thing after another until everything collapses—including ourselves. Exhausted and overwhelmed, we sit surrounded by tasks we need to do, obligations we need to meet, expectations we have to fulfill—so many need-tos and have-tos that we can almost hear a tiny voice inside us say, "See, I tried to warn you, but you didn't believe me! It's going to fall!"

Had the child known to lay a broad, firm foundation and limit how high she stacked the blocks, her tower wouldn't have fallen to the floor. Had we been wise enough to put God first, to make Him our foundation, and to follow His guidance as we took on our work, we wouldn't have ended up struggling to get through from morning to evening.

When you put God first—a set, regular prayer time, perhaps—you're laying a good foundation for the hours ahead. You're reminded why you're doing what you're doing…serving Him by serving others. You're in His presence, open to His will. You're receiving His peace, which holds up under even the heaviest burdens of the day.

Service Road

The block of granite which was an obstacle
in the pathway of the weak
becomes a stepping stone
in the pathway of the strong.

Thomas Carlyle

Just because God calls you to do something for others—say, work with underprivileged kids or help a frail neighbor with her housework—doesn't mean everything will magically fall into place. A few of the kids give you fits because they refuse to take responsibility for their actions. The neighbor criticizes the way you vacuum or doesn't seem to appreciate the hours you've spent helping her fill out a complex insurance form.

Though God has laid out a path for you, He never promised it would be smooth going! What He has promised, though, is a sure reward—and not just in the future, but now. These are only a few of His rewards for staying, for putting one foot in front of the other, even when you feel like giving up:

- Despite the frustrations, you possess the peace of mind known only to those who are fulfilling God's purpose for them in the things they do and say.
- Regardless of others' approval or disapproval, you experience life, gain experience, and grow in maturity and insight.
- Within the struggles and because of the struggles, you understand the struggles of others; and you strengthen your ability to see things through in your own life as you help others with their challenges.

Just ask anyone on the path ahead of you. Ask someone who has been selflessly serving others about the rewards of not giving up. Even more, ask God to take control of your feet—and your heart. Let Him shower His rewards on you!

Damage Control

When you go to bed at night,
have for your pillow three things–
love, hope and forgiveness.
And you will awaken in the morning
with a song in your heart.

Victor Hugo

Few of us are tempted to steal cars or rob banks, but we're still tempted to do the wrong thing. No, giving in to temptation might not make the headlines or land us in jail, but it's not without consequences. Consequences like ruined relationships...a damaged reputation...a burdened conscience.

We often opt to do the wrong thing under the illusion that we can control the outcome and that our actions really won't affect anyone to any measurable degree. A white lie will get us off the hook...a small deception will make things easier...a bit more for ourselves will never be missed. What temptation doesn't tell us, however, is what we discover for ourselves. We can't control the outcome. Though we never intended it, the white lie insulted our friend, who saw right through it. Our deception was discovered, and now no one trusts what we say. What we took mattered to another person. What we did lies heavy on our mind. We can't seem to forget.

God's forgiveness does more than lift the weight of guilt from us and give us the strength and motivation to put things right wherever possible. In addition, God's forgiveness takes the entire matter out of His sight.

Are you suffering from temptation? Let God introduce you to the ultimate in spiritual damage control!

Sincerely Right

Integrity without knowledge is weak and useless,
and knowledge without integrity is dangerous and dreadful.
Samuel Johnson

Genuine. Authentic. Heartfelt. All those words apply to someone who's sincere. Because we don't like being misled or feeling as if we're not hearing a person's true thoughts, we regard sincerity as an important plus in family members, friends, and coworkers. We aim for the same quality in ourselves.

Yet it's possible for someone—and ourselves—to be sincerely mistaken. Simply because we honestly feel something or strongly hold an opinion doesn't guarantee we're right. Our emotions can fool us into believing things are worse than they really are. Our opinions, though genuinely believed, may not reflect the facts. Then we find ourselves at odds with the world, struggling to make sense of what's happening around us.

Sincerity that brings peace and assurance, strength and commitment, is not based on our fleeting feelings or doubtful opinions, but flows from God's Spirit at work in our hearts. As we weave His timeless commandments into our daily lives, we come to know His truth. As we meet our challenges with God's guidance and help, we discover what's real, no matter what our feelings at the moment…and what's true, regardless of anyone's opinion (including our own).

Your sincerity is important, because sincerity enables and energizes. Sincerity has vitality and the power to change, manage, and accomplish things. That's why it matters so much what you're sincere about!

Enough Already!

You never know what is enough
unless you know what is more than enough.
William Blake

Most of us have experienced "more than enough"! From bygone Christmases and birthdays with more toys than we could enjoy in a lifetime of childhoods, to today's houses with maximum storage space for stuff we'll never use, we know "more than enough" quite well, and quite personally.

As we find out sooner or later, however, there's no lasting satisfaction in "more than enough." Though our possessions may be useful and practical, beautiful and valuable, up-to-date and top-of-the-line, we have no time to enjoy all of them. A goodly portion lay in boxes, stowed in closets, or sitting, unnoticed, on shelves or tabletops.

But perhaps it takes personal experience to truly convince us that more isn't necessarily better. When more things put more stress in our lives, they're not better. When too much to take care of means too little time to enjoy what we have, it's not better. When our focus is on getting more instead of sharing with others, we're not changing for the better.

God provides us with everything we need, and He graciously allows us more. He has put us in a place where we can enjoy comfort, pleasure, and even a measure of luxuries. And if we're willing to learn how to use our blessings for our well-being and the well-being of others, He will grant us the wisdom to know when to tell ourselves "enough."

Living Waters

We seek satisfaction in the baubles of the world,
yet we discover no satisfaction at all,
but only disappointment and despair.
Finding no solace anywhere, we at last turn to Reality,
where alone true satisfaction may be found.

Henry Thomas Hamblin

The summer sun rose hot, bright, and intense morning after morning. By late August, fields had browned, crops had withered, and animals were drifting listlessly in a futile search for shade. The old farm pond where three generations of kids had splashed and fished, pasturing cows had lapped, and countless birds had found food, now lay bone-dry under the searing sun.

It's a common scene when drought strikes farming communities. The image also serves as a picture of what happens spiritually when we get away from spending time with God in focused prayer, in attentive listening, and in thoughtful reflection. Our well of God-knowledge runs dry and the flowering of His presence in our lives becomes the memory of another season long ago. Where before there was joy and ease in His presence, now there is restlessness and distress as we wonder where He has gone—and if He will ever come again.

Though the farmer may wait and wait for the rain to make the fields fruitful again, you need never wait for the soothing, cleansing, and life-giving waters of God's presence. He is present to you now, ready to fill what is empty, heal what is hurting, and bring you fulfillment and abundance in Him.

Spiritual Living

The man who has no inner life is a slave to his surroundings, as the barometer is the obedient servant of the air.

Henri-Frédéric Amiel

If we're serious about excelling at sports or music or dance, we spend time—a lot of time!—in training. We regularly practice to build strength and agility...repeatedly perform drills, maneuvers, and movements so they'll become second nature...develop focus so we're not easily distracted...and thoroughly learn the rules and regulations of our craft so we can participate with competence. If we stop training, or fail to give it our best effort and full attention, our ability to perform will suffer.

Spiritual training isn't always as recognized or well-defined as physical and mental training, but it shares many of the same attributes. To advance spiritually, we're required to spend time with spiritual things, such as prayer, reading, and meditation. To build spiritual strength and agility, we apply what we've learned to our everyday lives in the way we respond to and interact with others.

For spiritual thinking and actions to become second nature, we constantly strive to do better with God's help. We learn to focus on God, not on the world's diversions. And yes, we thoroughly learn God's rules and regulations if we want to live a spiritual life of integrity and authenticity. Like a good coach or teacher, God knows what works and what doesn't. He shows us what lies within our control and what lies outside of our control so we can go forward with confidence and certainty.

If you're serious about spiritual life, let God, the giver of spiritual life, teach you how.

Time Now

Time is what we want most,
but what alas! we use worst.

William Penn

Suppose a friend of yours is at her wit's end trying to manage a busy family, a demanding job, and time-consuming committee meetings. After hearing her lament the fact that she has so little time for her husband or her two kids, you suggest that she mark off a family weekend for just the four of them. "Oh, no," she exclaims, "not until I get everything wrapped up at work and issues settled in my committees!"

You shake your head. She's losing her grip now, and it's relaxation away from work and meetings that she needs. It's family time now, not later, that will renew and restore her energy and remind her what's truly important in her life.

When life gets chaotic, however, and things start demanding more time, more energy, more attention, we drop daily time alone with God. We're in too much of a hurry! Sure, we know God is important, and it's not as if we're going to forget Him, it's just that right now, we're too busy. Later, we promise ourselves. Later! Just as soon as everything calms down, we'll get back to God. Yet the more harried we get, the less we're able to quiet ourselves in God's presence.

It's when things are hectic and hurried, muddled and confused that you most need the rest and refreshment God offers. Now, not later, you need to hear His voice and learn from Him what's most important in your life. He has given you time to spend time with Him.

Restless for a Reason

A single event can awaken within us
a stranger totally unknown to us.
Antoine de Saint-Exupéry

Ever feel at sixes and sevens? Sometimes it's a rainy Saturday morning when you just don't know what to do with yourself! It passes as soon as the sun comes out. But other times the mood persists for days or weeks or longer. That's when nothing satisfies, nothing works out, and nothing seems worth going after. You just don't know what to do with yourself! It's not a pleasant feeling, is it?

Restlessness, like an ache or pain, is a signal to you that something's wrong. It's often God's way of telling you that an aspect of your life needs attention. Used constructively, restlessness compels you to dig deeply into your current goals and values. Perhaps your actions undermine your professed objectives or go against the standards you say you support. Your restlessness might be a wake-up call for you to gain greater self-knowledge, rediscover your purpose, redefine your principles, or recalibrate your life's direction.

Like an ache or pain, some restlessness is merely temporary. It disappears with a little time out for a few stretches or a leisurely stroll around the block. But when restlessness persists, see it as a signal. There's a reason God is calling you for a little time out with you and Him alone.

His Good Plans

"For I know the plans I have for you," declares the LORD,
"plans to prosper you and not to harm you,
plans to give you hope and a future."
Jeremiah 29:11 NIV

Our fears and insecurities propel us in one of two directions. Our fears can cause us to pull away from life and all the opportunities open to us because we can't control the outcome. How do we know we won't fail miserably? Our insecurities can make us feel we don't deserve the blessings God has in store for us, so we don't reach out for them. We don't accept them. In this scenario, our fears and insecurities put us on a very lonely road!

Then again, our fears and insecurities can do just the opposite. Because we fear disappointment, we do everything we can to control the way things turn out for us. Leaving nothing to chance, we attempt to stage-manage every venture and manipulate anyone who has any influence over our lives or affects our place in the world. Though on the outside we look unshakable, inside we're quivering like a gelatin mold.

Of course you don't want to find yourself in either category—and neither does God. His answer to your fears and insecurities (we all have them!) rests in trust. Trust His protection and trust His ability to make you strong enough to get through any adversity that may come your way. Trust His love for you, and let His love lift your sense of self-esteem and self-worth. Trust His good plans for you.

Fortunate Misfortune

Man meets with adversity and fights it tooth and nail...
not knowing that it is merely a preparation for greater things
and a larger and fuller life.

Henry Thomas Hamblin

We may hate the situation we're in, but what can we do about it? We're supposed to make the best of it. We're expected to grin and bear it. We're told to look for the silver lining. But all the adages and tidbits of common wisdom do nothing to change our deepest thoughts, our inmost feelings.

If you've ever been in unhappy circumstances that you were powerless to change, you get the picture. Perhaps you lacked other opportunities, or you didn't have the influence or flexibility you would need to make things more to your liking. At least for a time, you had no meaningful control over where you were or how you spent your time.

Did you consider that God may have put you where you were for a reason? No, not to punish you or make you miserable, but for another reason. You were there because He had something for you to do, learn, explore, or experience—something that would make a difference for the better in your life or in the life of someone else. Perhaps there was an idea, a dream, a truth that He wanted to open up to you. Maybe He knew this would be the best place to discover more about yourself.

In God's plans, unpleasant or unfortunate circumstances could be the ones He's using to bring you closer to Him.

Right Place, Right Time

If God has wanted me otherwise,
He would have created me otherwise.
Johann Wolfgang von Goethe

Do you ever wonder why people—even strangers—tend to confide in you? That's because the gentleness and openness of your heart shows in the kindliness of your eyes and in the softness of your smile. Do you wonder why you're the one who's always asked to help out? That's because you're responsible and reliable, capable and fun to have around. Do you wonder…?

Actually, it's no wonder at all! God has given you more gifts, talents, and abilities than you know. Yes, some He uses in big parts of your life, but so many more He uses in small, everyday ways. He'll use your gift of cheerfulness to bring a smile to a stranger's face (didn't even see it, did you?). He'll use your talent for telling an amusing story or funny joke to lighten a friend's overburdened heart (no, you didn't know that's what you did). He'll use your ability to discern another's pain to prompt the question that brought a serious problem to light (and you thought you had simply asked).

Have you thanked God for all the blessings He has given others in you? You're doing nothing to plan or manage the little instances, but yes, there are those times when your heart tells you that you were in exactly the right place at exactly the right time.

Lucky or Blessed?

Chance is perhaps the pseudonym of God when He does not wish to sign His work.

Anatole France

Some people find it hard to believe in mere good luck. Why? Because some things have happened that they didn't plan, could never have foreseen, and couldn't have swayed in one direction or the other—yet worked a miracle in their lives. A casual meeting resulted in a valuable recommendation...a brief conversation led to a life-changing idea...a serendipitous choice worked into a fantastic opening.

Coincidence? It's hard to believe it's only coincidence when seemingly accidental events put us on the path to so many wonderful opportunities and awesome breaks. Some would say it's simple luck. Others might look more deeply...might pause and spend some time thinking about the odds that this would happen the way it did...that all the pieces, so up in the air not long ago, would come together in quite this way...this heartening, mysterious way.

If you're reflecting on the coincidences in your life (how many instances where it just had to be the hand of God?), go one step further. Enter into the wonder of God's will for you. Yes, it's marvelous. Yes, it's mysterious. And yes, it reminds you that, as brilliantly as you could have taken control and made things work out your way...wasn't it brilliant—super-brilliant—the way God did it?

Some might call it good luck, but perhaps a better way to put it is "very blessed." You are very blessed.

Pressure Points

Consider how much more you often suffer
from your anger and grief,
than from those very things for which
you are angry and grieved.

Marcus Antonius

How about a multiple choice quiz? Try this one:

I'm most likely to tell them what I think when:

a. They walk away from the dinner table and leave me with all the clean-up to do.
b. I'm expected to be available to shuttle them from school to games, lessons, and friends' houses 24/7.
c. I look around the room and realize that I'm the one doing most of the work.
d. All of the above.

For many of us, the answer is "d"! We have our pressure points, and resentment has taken root. In fact, now that we're focused on it, we realize that we've been cultivating low-, medium-, or even high-level resentment for quite a while.

Resentment, like a weed, sows more resentment in your heart and mind. When does it stop? Not when you tell them what you think, but when you tell God. Don't worry, He won't cringe! Instead, He'll listen and care. Your time with Him will open you to His help and guidance.

Remaining in His presence, eliminate resentment by reclaiming control of your time where you can, and by accepting circumstances where you can't, or decide not to. There are things you can delegate to someone else…bow out of…continue doing, but with a sprinkle of good humor and the flow of laughter. It's your choice, and that makes all the difference.

An Invitation to Love

Be still, and know that I am God.

Psalm 46:10

Our definition of love changes and develops with time. For children, love often comes simply and without question—say, their love for their parents or their devotion to a favorite teacher or caring relative. Teens might describe love as a volatile emotion, but later, as we experience more of life and relationships, we learn that love is much, much more. It's commitment, even when the going gets rough. It's caring, even if it would be easier to ignore or overlook. Love is love, even without the sensation or excitement of being *in* love.

Including all this and beyond all this is the kind of love God invites you to experience with Him. He asks for a simple, childlike love that gives you the boldness to come to Him with anything at any time. Yet there's feeling involved—heart-deep feeling—that affects how you think of God and reflects in your love for others.

There's also caring and commitment from Him to you that never changes, no matter how many times you have wavered or grown cold. It's this kind of love that burns steady, even if you don't feel loved or loving right now. God's love is there. It will never fail you.

Enter into His love. His door is always open. Imagine yourself welcomed, invited to sit down, asked what you would like. Let Him serve you with His all-encompassing love.

The Right Fit

There is just one life for each of us: our own.

Euripides

"One size fits all," the label reads. But when you try on one-size-fits-all clothing, you may find that while the garment may fit many people, one size doesn't fit all. When it comes to the values you want to live by and the choices you make, the same holds true. Your values and choices might look like those of many, but one size doesn't fit all. It's up to you to find the right fit for you.

Many of us find ourselves overcommitted and overwhelmed because we have taken a one-size-fits-all approach to life. What others are doing, we do. What others at our age and stage in life are choosing, we choose. If social commentators, public figures, and admired celebrities say this is what we should value, we go right along. Before we know it, we're "wearing" a life that doesn't fit!

You know it doesn't fit the same way you know a garment doesn't fit. A constant train of obligations trailing after you like a long, crooked hem...strain at the seams of days packed with too much to do...an uncomfortable pull as you reach for goals and objectives that aren't what you really want. Isn't it time to change clothes?

God has something for you that's exactly your size. In His purpose for your life, you'll find your niche. It might not be what everyone else is wearing, or even most people like you are wearing, but it will be yours. And it will fit you to a T...guaranteed!

Completely Nuts!

Be glad of life because it gives you the chance to love, and to work, and to play, and to look up at the stars.

Henry van Dyke

What drives you nuts? For some of us, it's automatic answering machines and self-service check-out stations. For others among us, it's rush-hour traffic (as if anyone could really rush at that pace!) and discourteous drivers. And how about loud music in restaurants and long lines—anyplace? Each one of us could make a long list of what's wrong with the world!

But how about another approach—a long list of what's right with the world. Loving families and supportive friends…warm feelings and heart-deep laughter…shared stories and great times to remember long after. There are sunny skies and leafy trees, newly opened roses and the sweet scent of lilac on the wind. And how about the aroma of fresh coffee and a feel of rich, melty chocolate on the tip of your tongue? And oh yes…nuts. The kind sprinkled on top of a tall ice cream sundae (as long as you're not allergic to them)!

You might not be able to do anything at all about what's on your list of things that drive you nuts, but you can decide to not let them drive you very far. Get in control of the wheel by thinking about what's right with the world. What's right with the world makes not only a longer list, but a livelier and happier one.

When it's your own doubts, fears, or anxieties that are driving you nuts, here's something else to think about. God invites you to give Him the wheel. Turn over to Him what you have done wrong and think, instead, of what He has done right. The list is endless. So start yours now for a livelier and happier you. You're really going places now!

Let nothing disturb you,
Let nothing frighten you.
All things are passing,
God only is changeless.
Patience gains all things.
Who has God wants nothing...
God alone suffices.

Teresa of Avila

It's OK

I've got Everything under control.

-God

Devotions, Encouragement & Reminders that He's Always There

Inspired by Faith

It's OK... I've got Everything under control. -God

ISBN 978-0-9886719-7-3

Published by Product Concept Mfg., Inc.
2175 N. Academy Circle #200, Colorado Springs, CO 80909

Written and Compiled by Patricia Mitchell
in association with Product Concept Mfg., Inc.

All scripture quotations are from the King James version of the Bible unless otherwise noted.

Sayings not having a credit listed are contributed by writers for Product Concept Mfg., Inc. or in a rare case, the author is unknown.